GIBBONS
The Invisible Apes

John Steckley

PHOTOGRAPHS AND ILLUSTRATIONS
BY ANGELIKA STECKLEY

Rock's Mills Press
Oakville, Ontario

PUBLISHED BY

Rock's Mills Press

Copyright © 2015 by John Steckley
PUBLISHED BY ARRANGEMENT WITH THE AUTHOR • ALL RIGHTS RESERVED

Library and Archives Canada Cataloguing in Publication is available from the publisher. Email Rock's Mills Press at customer.service@rocksmillspress.com.

Cover photograph by Angelika Steckley

ISBN-13: 978-1-77244-007-2

Contents

Gibbons

Introduction

Why did I decide to write a book about gibbons? That's a good question, especially as I have never written a book about animals before.

I will begin by saying that I am a big supporter of the underdog, or in this case the "under-ape"—though perhaps that's not quite the right term, given how high up in the trees that gibbons live, just one of the things you will learn in the pages ahead. It seems to me that books are typically written and documentaries made about the "usual subjects." Such subjects are worth talking about, surely, but what about those topics that are not mentioned, that are more often than not ignored? Those are the kinds of subjects that appeal to me most. For instance, I have spent most of my life researching and writing about an Aboriginal language, Wendat (Huron), which long ago lost its last speaker, and had no one writing about it. Once I learned that it had no speakers, but that there was lots of unpublished material written in and about the language in the 17th and 18th centuries, it seemed the right thing to do to plunge into the deep end and learn about and write (five books so far, two more coming out soon) all that I could about the Wendat language.

The other reason is gibbons themselves. My wife Angie and I are both easily charmed by charming animals. We own eight parrots, two dogs and a cat named Brenda. We feed a family of fat squirrels (Dani and her children) on our front ledge. They live in a front yard where many different kinds of wild birds (sparrows, blue jays, starlings, mourning doves, chickadees, and so on), one arthritic raccoon, a possum, some rabbits, and most recently some mice like to feed. We go to Stratford, Ontario to visit and feed corn by hand to the swans, geese and ducks there. It was in character with that fascination and connection with animals that we got charmed by the small apes. They created a space in our hearts that we soon filled with long arms and furry faces. I originally visited just one zoo to gather material for a paragraph or two on gibbons for an anthropology textbook that I was writing. I did not originally intend to write any more on the subject. The apes made me do it.

How Are Gibbons Invisible?

Why are we calling this book *Gibbons: The Invisible Apes*? It is because gibbons *are* invisible in the West, meaning Europe and especially North America. The big organizations that represent and advocate for animals, particularly endangered animals, do not speak or write about or show pictures of gibbons. They prefer to talk about the already known, the familiar. We have found that in zoos gibbons are not represented well—few big signs indicate their presence, few pictures on websites show you what they look like, few stuffed toys can be bought in zoo gifts shops, few special projects are engaged in, and no books about them are available. In both cases gibbons live in the very big shadows of the "great" apes: gorillas, orangutans (especially these guys, as they share some of the same habitat and countries of origin), chimpanzees, and bonobos (although these chimpanzee lookalikes are a little invisible themselves).

Even when people do see gibbons in zoos, the furry creatures' identity as apes remains invisible. They are small and therefore for zoo visitors, children and their parents alike, gibbons must be monkeys. When I retire I am thinking about hanging around gibbon compounds in zoos and informing people, "They are not monkeys, they are gibbons!" And maybe I will also put up a few homemade signs with that important message. Graffiti for gibbons! That sounds like a good cause to me.

CHAPTER ONE

Gibbons: The Invisible Apes

White-handed and black-furred, with a bewitching black-and-white face, the gibbon known as Penelope, Penny or Miss P. of the Bowmanville Zoo in southern Ontario may be small in size—five pounds and growing slowly when I met her in 2010, she is twice that weight now—but her presence is big when you stand before her compound. And it isn't just her very thick fur and her very long arms that fill you with her presence. You can't miss her as she swings from branch to branch in her zoo compound, or as she seeks you out, turning her little face towards you as she hangs from her long-fingered hands intertwined in the mesh links that separate ape from human. Even when she is sitting on the ground, her face turned both shyly and slyly in your direction, you are filled with her presence. And yet, in broad social terms, she is invisible.

Invisibility and Gibbons
Penelope, like all gibbons, can be called an invisible ape. Why might that be so? As an anthropologist-observer of the relationship between humans and other animals, I call gibbons invisible because many people do not see them for what they are. I believe that when most people in the West see a gibbon in a zoo, they think they see a *monkey*. For gibbons are monkey-sized, not up to the usual ape bulk and build of their larger cousins, the "great apes." Even Charles Darwin, in his *Descent of Man* (1859), once referred to gibbons as monkeys, stating: "The gibbons are the noisiest of the monkeys." Darwin knew gibbons were apes, and made a point of distinguishing between apes and monkeys elsewhere in the text. This was just a rare moment of carelessness on his part.

How do you avoid gibbon blindness? How do you know you're observing an ape and not a monkey when you're looking at a gibbon? The easiest and most basic criterion is what I (as a long-time teacher) call the tail test. Monkeys have tails. Like humans and the other apes (orangutans, gorillas, chimpanzees, and bonobos), gibbons have a tailbone, but no tail. There are cheaters, however, on this test: the Barbary macaque and the misleadingly named Celebes ape. The first is a primate found in Algeria and Morocco, and even sometimes in Gibraltar, on the European side of the Mediterranean. As it has a small stub of a tail, this tricky monkey has been commonly and incorrectly called the Barbary ape. The Celebes ape (the name that invariably appears on their cage when they are in zoos) possesses an even smaller stump. But it is a monkey. The Celebes "ape" has a tail.

How else are gibbons invisible? Their presence in zoos is often obscured in a number of unintentional but still effective ways. Zoo websites

tend to hide gibbons away in the back web pages (if they show them at all), not on the home page. The Mogo Zoo in Australia is a refreshing exception, with a picture of one of their siamangs front and centre on their home page. The general absence of signs marked *gibbon* when you physically visit zoos also makes gibbons invisible until such time as you're actually looking into their cage. Big signs directing you around a zoo often tell you where you can go to see the great apes, which are the big guys: gorillas, orangutans and chimpanzees. They do not often point to gibbons, the so-called lesser apes. Again there are wonderful exceptions. One of them is Safari Niagara in Fort Erie, in southern Ontario. A reasonably big sign there declares the gibbons' presence.

Gibbons are invisible in zoo gift stores as well. Very few cards, posters, T-shirts, plush toys and figurines represent gibbons. And when these are available, there is often no reference to what they are. By default, most people will think they are monkeys. Recently during a visit to a zoo, I changed that for a short period of time by writing on a sheet of paper "These are gibbons," and sticking my hastily made sign on the stand from which gibbon plush toys were hanging from their long arms. I am not recommending that children do this, only "mature" adults.

Don't, however, let the term *lesser ape* influence your opinion regarding the abilities of these remarkable creatures. "Lesser" merely refers to size. That's why some researchers (and this author) today call gibbons *small* rather than lesser apes. Gibbons are big on personality, activity, and speed, as well as general mobility. In fact, you could say gibbons are the Olympians of their habitat. And, as we will see later, there are more species of gibbons than of all the other apes put together. As gibbon guru Thomas Geissmann states, "roughly seventy percent of all ape species are gibbons." By my calculations (counting the two species each of gorillas, chimpanzees and orangutans, plus one each of humans and bonobos), he is right, as the currently calculated percentage is 68%.

Yet despite that impressive statistic, college students I've taught over the past 30 years typically neglect to mention gibbons when asked to name members of the ape sub-order. Gibbons are invisible to them, too. I feel confident in saying my students are not forgetting about gibbons when I ask them that question. They never learned gibbons existed in the first place. It's an ignorance built into our culture, an unfortunate facet of Western learning about animals. Generally we in the West do not do not film gibbons, study gibbons, or write easily readable books or articles about gibbons.

Even the movie *Planet of the Apes* and its sequels helped to make gibbons invisible. In the first movie the chimps (including a hero and heroine) were the intellectuals and the scientists. The gorillas were the enforcers, the police, military and the man-hunters. The orangutans were the administrators, politicians and lawyers. Where were the gibbons? On the planet of the lesser apes?

The popular literature about gibbons is lacking. You can easily see this if you engage in an Internet search on the subject, or put in "gibbons" as a search term on Amazon. You will discover that there are many authors named "Gibbon," and little else. And yet there is good scientific material out there, and has been for quite some time. There are champions of gibbons active both in the academic world and the conservation movement— Thomas Geissmann, David Chivers, Danielle Whittaker, Susan Lappan, Alan Mootnick and Shirley McGreal. But they do not write books for the popular market. These authors and scientists are busy enough discovering and recording previously neglected information about gibbons and running much-needed rescue centres and sanctuaries. All of them have provided much needed background research for this book.

For the gibbons there hasn't been a popular champion like Jane Goodall of the chimpanzees, no Dian Fossey of the gorillas or Biruté Galdikas of the orangutans. Even baboons, which can be classed as monkeys, have recently had a best-seller written about them by Dorothy L. Cheney and Robert M. Seyfarth: *Baboon Metaphysics: The Evolution of a Social Mind*. And there is Robert Sapolsky's *A Primate's Memoir*, which includes some wonderful baboon stories.

Now think. Have you ever read an article about gibbons in *National Geographic*? I know that you haven't, as there hasn't been one that I can find. Have you ever seen a documentary on the plight of the gibbons, or signed an e-mail petition to help save the gibbons? Again your answer will be in the negative. They are invisible in these places, unlike their larger cousins, who, fortunately for them, are also large in the media.

Gibbons are also almost completely invisible in English fiction. That is bad enough, but they are constantly being upstaged by those pushy orangutans. For example, hoolocks are the types of gibbons that live in India. Yet in Rudyard Kipling's *Jungle Book*, the ape featured in the story about wildlife in India was an orangutan, not a gibbon. And orangutans don't even live in India. Kipling's father, John Lockwood Kipling, did write about them briefly in *Beast and Man in India: A Popular Sketch of Indian Animals in Their Relation to the People*. Maybe the son never read his father's book. Neither of my sons have read any of mine (I hope this will be an exception).

A rare exception to this no-gibbons rule in fiction comes from historical novelist Patrick O'Brian. In the second book of his acclaimed series about Captain Jack Aubrey, *Post Captain* (1972), he mentions Cassandra, a gibbon who swings aboard ship while it's docked in a Burmese port. When Jack first sees her swinging through the masts and sails, he thinks it's one of his crew falling horribly to his death. Then she executes an amazing maneuver no human sailor could pull off. He asks crew members who's aloft, and discovers poor Cassandra is often drunk because she's constantly fed rum from the sailors' daily rations. Unfortunately, the Wikipedia entry on the book does not include Cassandra in the list of characters, invisible again.

Recently, Justin D'Ath, a children's and young adult writer from Australia, has published the second volume of his *The Lost World Circus* series, entitled *The Singing Ape*. You will read about that charming aspect of gibbons' nature in the second chapter. Perhaps D'Ath could write a sequel entitled *The Swinging Ape*, an exciting aspect of gibbons also covered in the next chapter.

Visibility in the East

While gibbons have little prominence in the culture of the West, in South Asia (India and Bangladesh) and Southeast Asia (Burma, Laos, Cambodia, Thailand, Vietnam, China, Malaysia and Indonesia) gibbons have long been celebrated in stories and artwork. Centuries of poetry celebrate their often mournful-sounding singing heard high in the trees, echoing through mountains and valleys. Unfortunately, an amazing and beautiful book showcasing Chinese poetry, artwork and stories about gibbons, Robert Hans van Gulik's *The Gibbon in China: An Essay in Chinese Animal Lore* (1967), shares with the gibbons its near invisibility. I have only seen a few passages online. If I thought that more than a very few of the readers of this book could have access to it, I would recommend it along with the six other books on gibbons discussed on pages 147–48.

In *The Sacred Monkeys of Bali*, an important work in the interdisciplinary field of *cultural primatology* (involving the study of the relationships between human groups and other primates in different cultural traditions), Bruce P. Wheatley discusses how greatly various Eastern traditions differ from Western ones in the respect given to other primates. This he exemplifies with monkeys (the subject of his book) being addressed with the Japanese honorific *san*, usually used after the name or kinship relationship as signs of address for older or more powerful humans. Monkeys were considered as having souls, and even as being deities in the character of *Hanuman* of traditional Indian and Indonesian belief. A similar situation existed with gibbons.

Gibbon stories abound in the countries where they live. The following stories come from Thailand and Malaysia.

Gibbon Theatre

In Thailand there is a traditional form of theatre called *likay*. It includes singing, dancing, elaborate costumes (including masks), a lot of makeup, a little improvisation, Bollywood Thai-style and humour. A story long celebrated in *likay* is the tale of Prince Chantakorop and Mora. It will be told in a more Western style with my own brand of humour.

Prince Chantakorop was sent out by his parents to learn of the magic in the world from a hermit monk. The monk did not live alone. His lovely daughter lived with him. Do you see where this is going? She entertained and enchanted the prince with her dancing (cue a Bollywood-style dance scene).

When Chantakorop's studies with the monk were completed, he prepared to leave to return to the palace where he would soon become king. Before he left, the monk presented to him the gift of a large clay urn. It was given with the following words:

> Within this urn is a gift I hope you will treasure forever. It contains your heart's greatest desire. However, you may not open the urn until you reach your father's palace. If you open it before you have reached the safety of your own kingdom, great misfortune will befall you.

The prince vowed to obey the hermit's warning, but his curiosity burned like the coals of a recent fire. And, of course, we (and certainly the audience) know what (or should we say who?) is in the urn.

Chantakorop bid his mentor farewell. As each day passed in the prince's long walk through the jungle, the prince's curiosity grew. Finally,

"Pua, pua, pua"

he could wait no longer. He impatiently removed the lid from the urn. Much to his (but not our) surprise, Mora, the monk's beautiful daughter, magically appeared before him. Cue another dance scene, with much singing.

Chantakorop and Mora were married in the nearest village. Eager to present his bride to his father, the prince hurriedly continued his journey toward the royal palace with his new wife. Say, wasn't there a warning that he violated somewhere along the way?

Before they arrived at the safety of the palace, a bandit appeared, sword in hand, challenging the prince to a fight. Lovely Mora would be the prize. A long swordfight/dance routine follows in the traditional presentation. Then the bandit strikes a decisive blow, knocking the valiant prince down, his sword beyond his reach. He cries out, "Mora! Quickly, if you cherish my life, bring me my sword!"

Mora reached for the sword. She was momentarily distracted by the dazzling sight of the bold (and beautiful) bandit and left the sword where it lay. The bandit then seized the weapon for himself and killed the prince in an instant. Shocked by the result of her brief instant of indecision, Mora bent over the body of her beloved prince and cried, "Pua, pua, pua (husband, husband, husband)."

The bandit took the heartbroken Mora away. She went with him, but all she could do the entire time was sadly call out, "Pua, pua, pua." As sunset approached, the monk suddenly appeared before his daughter and the bandit. Ashamed of his daughter's betrayal, he turned her into a white-handed gibbon. Today, when you hear the lonesome gibbon call of "Pua, pua, pua" in the jungle, it is the remorseful Mora, singing in eternal regret. A little song, a little dance, and a little ape swinging from a branch.

Going Ape Over a Man: Princess Telan Becomes a Siamang

The resemblance of siamang gibbons to humans makes these relatively large gibbons (around twice the weight of other gibbon species) a ready source of shape-shifting stories. Here is one such story.

In times far past, Princess Telan was engaged to be married to a man named Si Malim Bongsu. The period of their engagement was to be some three to four months. Shortly after his successful proposal, Bongsu sailed away and was gone longer than the promised four months.

Bongsu's elder brother, Si Malim Panjang, knew an opportunity when he spotted one, so he proposed to Princess Telan. When she turned him down, he became violent. To escape him, she turned into a siamang and escaped into the jungle canopy. But she missed her fiancé, so she climbed up into a tall tree that grew beside the sea. She called out to him saying: "You have broken your solemn promise and engagement, and I have to take upon myself the form of an ape." An unusual choice, you might think, but not in Malaysian stories.

As it turns out, Bongsu, who had returned and just happened to be passing by at the time, recognized her voice. Somewhat strangely, he took a blow-gun and shot her, causing her to fall into the sea. Then, perhaps realizing who she was, he took rosewater and sprinkled it over her fallen body, so that she became human again. They travelled together, but still he did not wed her, promising her that he would do so after coming back from another trip. Of course, he had made that promise before and look what happened. . . .

9

A little suspicious this time, she declared: "If you do not return within three months, you will find me turned into an ape." Events repeated themselves. The elder brother tried again to charm his younger brother's fiancé, and again she turned herself into a siamang as a somewhat strange way of saying "no." Again her fiancé stayed away longer than the promised period. Again she cried out in complaint concerning how he had forced her to yet again become a siamang (although when she made that cry, she had changed back into a human, at least momentarily). Again Bongsu passed by, and heard her cry. This time, he cried out, "Better it were for me I be nothing but a big fish." He leapt into the water, disappeared and was changed into a big fish. Be careful what you wish for (or what you fish for).

Princess Telan and her nurse were bathing at the time. Shocked and surprised by the fiancé's actions, they both became animals, the princess a siamang, the nurse a Malaysian sun bear. They changed so fast they didn't have time to rinse off the soap they had been washing with. It remained on their chests and eyebrows. And so they remain to this day.

One anthropological footnote should be added to this story. Western scientists typically describe siamangs as being coloured all black. That is accurate in most but not all cases. Recently, leading gibbon researcher Thomas Geissmann discovered that some siamangs, especially females, have white eyebrows, and suggested that this might be an ancient siamang feature, though not one noted by Western researchers. It seems from the story just told that Malaysians noticed a long time ago that some females have those white markings. I learned as an anthropologist that you should never underestimate the traditional knowledge of an ancient people. Western science sometimes documents much later what traditional peoples already knew. This is often seen in relation to medicines and in general knowledge about plants and animals. Canadian anthropologist Wade Davis often writes on that subject, especially in his book *Light at the Edge of the World*.

Eastern representation of gibbons is not restricted to theatre and stories. For hundreds of years in China and Japan, gibbons have been major subjects of artwork, as common as wolves, bears, loons and eagles are in pictures drawn in the Europe and North America. But this work has not attracted a significant audience in the West. Again, there is that invisibility turning up where it is not wanted. My wife Angie's hard work in learning how to draw gibbons (particularly their faces) is a much valued part of this book. She had to learn how to do it all on her own. But look to the end of the chapter to see her guide to drawing gibbon faces.

The Story So Far

What I hope you've learned from this chapter is that gibbons are culturally constructed as being invisible in Western culture, where they are only seen in zoos—and even then often only "seen" as monkeys—and sanctuaries. But that's not the case in the East, where people have long experienced gibbons in the wild. It might, however, be more to the point to say that the gibbon image has yet to be constructed in the West. Scientists have been writing the blueprints, giving us information that would be highly useful in learning about this wonderful small ape. So far, though, textbooks, novels, movies, documentaries and libraries do not provide people in the West with stories and images that can make gibbons visible in our culture. Few gibbon drawings decorate the walls of school classrooms. In the chapters that follow we will be following the scientific blueprints, but, to finally conclude this extended metaphor, adding a few individual flourishes of gibbons that I have met or that others have found fascinating. They are certainly worth getting to know. A clear image of gibbons will emerge, and they will never be invisible to you again. I hope that will enable you to construct a picture that you in turn can pass on to others and, in doing so, help end gibbon invisibility!

Giving Gibbons a Face

Do you want to draw the fact of a gibbon? It is not quite like that of a monkey or a chimp. Here is a method so foolproof that even I, a writer but not an artist, can do it.

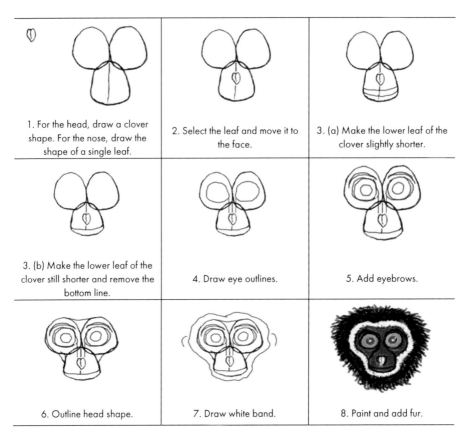

1. For the head, draw a clover shape. For the nose, draw the shape of a single leaf.

2. Select the leaf and move it to the face.

3. (a) Make the lower leaf of the clover slightly shorter.

3. (b) Make the lower leaf of the clover still shorter and remove the bottom line.

4. Draw eye outlines.

5. Add eyebrows.

6. Outline head shape.

7. Draw white band.

8. Paint and add fur.

This face will stay with you for a while.

CHAPTER TWO

Some Basic Gibbon Facts

Y ou now know a few basic facts about gibbons, a lot more than what your family members and friends probably know. Gibbons do not have tails, so they are apes and not monkeys, even though they are monkey-sized. They are invisible in the West where they are foreigners, but visible in the East where their homeland is. Now you are ready for a longer list of basic gibbon facts. If there were to be a test, these facts would be on it.

What is a Gibbon?
We have established a gibbon is not a monkey, but rather a small ape. Of course, it is an animal, and therefore belongs to the scientific kingdom Animalia, just like worms, trout, salamanders, turtles, parrots, dogs, Barbary macaques, chimps and humans. And like us, but unlike worms, gibbons have a backbone, which means they belong to the phylum Chordata. Like dogs, Barbary macaques, chimps and humans, gibbons are mammals (class: Mammalia). Like Barbary macaques, chimps and humans, gibbons are primates (order: Primata). Like chimps and humans, gibbons are hominoids (meaning "like a human"; sub-Order: Hominoidea). Different from all the others, gibbons belong to the family Hylobatidae (i.e., are hylobatids), a separation from the other apes (including humans) that is generally believed to have occurred some 15 million years ago. Before that there might have been a common ape ancestor. It would have looked a little like all apes, but also a little different, as it *was* an ancestor. Apes alive today have had another 15 million years to evolve. All of us have come a long way since then.

So what does that relationship mean in terms of genetics? The characteristics and potential of every living creature are spelled out by its *genes*, the aggregations of DNA molecules that are gathered together in bodies called *chromosomes* that are found in the central part (the *nucleus*) of living cells. The full grouping of genes for an individual or species is called its *genome*. How much are we genetically alike? Humans and gibbons share some 95% of our genomes, as opposed to the 98.4% we share with chimpanzees and bonobos, the 97.7% in common with gorillas, and the 96.4% in common with orangutans. With those big monkeys that are baboons, we share about 90%. To keep this in context of other living entities, I have read in award-winning Scottish poet Gillian K. Ferguson's *The Human Gene: Poems on the Book of Life* that we share 75% of our genes with pumpkins, and 57% with cabbages. I've never thought of a cabbage as particularly intelligent, but they do have heads. Pumpkins I can more readily identify with. At least I have seen some of them smile late in October. But it can be an evil smile.

The family name *Hylobatidae* comes from a Greek word meaning "dweller in the trees," which describes gibbons pretty well.

Put all this information in a list and we have the following:

Classification	Latin Term	English Term
Kingdom	Animalia	Animals
Phylum	Chordata	Chordates
Class	Mammalia	Mammals
Order	Primata	Primates
Superfamily	Hominoidea	Hominoids, apes
Family	Hylobatidae	Hylobates, gibbons

What are the basic physical features that make up a gibbon? Here are some fundamental characteristics—their top ten traits (as judged by me):

Top Ten Traits
SHARED PRIMATE TRAITS
1. Gibbons have their eyes on the front of their head, not on the sides. Seeing the same things from slightly different angles enables them (and us) to see distances well, say between them and the nearest branch. This is called *stereoscopic* or *3-D vision*. Cats have their eyes in a similar position, and they, too, are good in the trees. Having a small nose helps too, as it

14

does not block the centre of sight. Our border collie Wiikwaas has a big nose and eyes more on the side of his head than ours are. He bumps into chair legs a lot, and is generally not well-constructed for life in the trees.

2. Gibbons have five fingers, and more of a thumb than your dog or cat has. A gibbon's thumb appears lower down their hand than ours does. They swing from branches on four fingers. And unlike with our feet, their big toe sticks out ready to grab something. I would like that ability as I am too big and old to enjoy bending over to pick things up.

SHARED HOMINOID TRAIT

3. Gibbons do not have tails. You've read that before.

HYLOBATID TRAITS

4. Gibbons are very furry, with a density of fur that is much thicker than the fur of other apes (especially us, the naked apes), and roughly twice the density of a monkey's fur. This is one major reason why they look heavier and generally larger than they actually are.

5. Gibbons are small for apes (usually 10 to 15 pounds for an adult, except for siamangs, who range to about twice that weight).

6. They are territorial. The size of the area occupied by a family varies. In Feeroz and Islam's excellent *Ecology and Behaviour of the Hoolocks of Bangladesh* (1992), they describe a family group that had a home territory of 32 hectares, roughly 80 acres, about mid-sized for a gibbon family. It is the size of a small farm. Gibbon expressions of territoriality are relatively non-violent, when compared to that of other apes. Mostly they just sing and shout at intruders.

7. Gibbons are fundamentally *monogamous* (from the Greek words "mono," meaning "one," and "gam," meaning "marriage."). That means that they typically form long-lasting pairs when they mate, with one male and one female. Typically they mate for life

8. They live (i.e., eat, travel, play and sleep) in the trees.

9. They sing (mostly duets).

10. They swing, farther and faster than anyone.

BRACHIATION

Let's take that last point first. If gibbons were much more well-known, they would be famous for their world-leading ability to swing in the trees or *brachiate* (based on the Latin term *brachium*, meaning *arm*). Here are some basic questions and answers regarding gibbon brachiation.

Q: How far can gibbons swing from branch to branch?

A: They can brachiate up to a distance of 15 metres or roughly 50 feet. Remember, they are travelling downwards as well as horizontally. Still, that is impressive. It is the width of an NBA or college regulation basketball court. Two such swings would surpass the length of the court by about six feet. Seven swings would make the distance of a home run in most major league fields.

Q: How fast can gibbons move when they brachiate?

A: Different figures are given for this. The fastest I have read was that gibbons can brachiate up to 56 kilometres an hour or 35 miles per hour. They are the fastest non-flying creatures in the trees. If gibbons brachiated over the road that leads to the college where I teach, where the speed limit is 40 kph, and the police caught them with a radar gun, they would get a ticket for speeding: "But officer, I never touched the ground!"

Q: Do they ever crash?

A: Yes, it is not uncommon for gibbons to break bones because of brachiation error. Fortunately, their light weight and thick fur help keep the breakage to a minimum. In his classic study on the subject, "Notes on Disease and Healed Fractures of Wild Apes," early primatologist Adolph Schultz noted that of 118 "collected" (unfortunately that means shot and studied) adult gibbons, 36% had healed fractures, with 14% having multiple fractures. Almost one-quarter of those fractures were of the humerus (the bone that goes from your elbow to your shoulder) or femur (the bone that goes from your knee to your butt), suggesting that the injuries came from falls.

Q: How far can they jump? (This isn't brachiation, but it is still impressive.)

A: From a standing position a fit gibbon can jump up to 8 metres or 27 feet. The running long jump world record for humans is 8.95 metres or 29.4 feet. The human standing long jump record is 3.71 metres, less than half the length that the much smaller gibbons can jump.

Q: What gives gibbons the ability to brachiate (or, in other words, why can't I brachiate too)?

A: There are several good reasons why gibbons can brachiate so well and we can't. One is their arms are much longer than their legs. For example, a silvery gibbon's arms vary between 44 to 48 centimetres (17.3 to 19.3 inches) in length. That's about 25% longer than their legs. Think of it like this. If you had those proportions and you tried to walk as you normally do, your hands might drag on the ground. However, you would have a distinct advantage in shooting pool.

Another reason gibbons can brachiate so well is they are much lighter than humans. Most species of gibbons have adult males and females weighing only ten to 14 pounds. You, the non-brachiating human reader, weigh at least ten times that. The ground would be very fast in greeting you.

Additionally, gibbons' hands and forearms are proportionately much longer than a human's, so they can get a better grip on a branch, and use their forearms as somewhat like a slingshot. Most gibbon species grab a branch by hooking their four fingers around it.

Lastly, gibbons have a ball and socket joint in their wrists, similar to the ball and socket joint in the shoulders of humans and other primates, which makes the gibbons' wrist act more like a rotating joint than a hinge. It meets the stress with flexibility, not just strength.

SINGING

Gibbons can sing, with voices that you cannot forget! Ancient Chinese poets and musicians long took inspiration from these songs. In the fourth century A.D. Yüan Sung wrote:

> In the gorges [deep valleys] the calls of the gibbon are extremely clear, mountains and valleys resound with the echo, a deeply sad, continuous wailing. Travellers sung it in the words:
> Sad the calls of the gibbons at the three gorges of Pa-tung;
> After three calls in the night, tears wet the (travellers') [clothes].

More gruesome (maybe that's why I like it) but still poetic is a sixth-century poet's lines, where the then-popular Chinese images of the crane (the water bird) and the gibbon are paired:

> The crane's call is of utter loneliness
> The gibbon's song cuts through the entrails.

I have heard gibbons singing a good number of times. I have always been fascinated, but my entrails are intact. Fortunately, poetic license includes metaphor.

Gibbons have different songs to sing. Each species has its own songs. Some songs are species-specific; that is, only gibbons of that species will sing those particular songs. Some songs are learned, at least in part. If you were a gibbon of one species and were raised by gibbons of another species, you might include some song traits of your adopted parents.

In 2009, when my wife Angie and I first visited the white-handed gibbons in the Toronto Zoo—Lenny and Holly—we were told that because the two of them had been raised with gibbons of mixed species, they had a mixed collection of songs. This would be rather like being able to sing opera and jazz music at more or less the same time.

Even though I had often read about the songs, I still was not completely prepared for the powerful effect gibbon singing would have on me. In my experience it does haunt you when you first hear it, and every subsequent time, too. Let me tell you about our first experience.

When Angie and I went to Jungle Cat World in Orono, Ontario, we heard our first gibbon duet. I definitely had to struggle to describe what we heard. Metaphors and similes failed. The two singers were Samson (the older brother of Penelope, who is on the cover of this book) and Carmen. The most dramatic part of the song I described as being like a fireworks rocket going off, rising from lower to higher pitch, ending with a whistle. Not a bad description of the sounds, but not a particularly good one, either. Samson and Carmen's duet lasted only about two or three minutes, which is short for a gibbon song. Normally songs average about 15 to 20 minutes. That would be way too long for play on the radio.

What made Samson and Carmen's song especially dramatic was they did not sing alone. Shortly after the two gibbons started their duet, another duet came in response, not from gibbons, but from two young wolves howling from the far side of the zoo. They may have come from opposite ends of the world (Canada and Southeast Asia), but the two different species could still sing together.

Ask anyone who works at a zoo that has a gibbon population, and you will hear about how the little guys sing in the morning.

MONOGAMY

One of the best known aspects of gibbons is their monogamy. For people easily disturbed by bonobo and chimpanzee promiscuity, and by silverback gorilla harems, gibbons have been socially comforting. They have played the role of "paragons of fidelity" and according to Whittaker and Lappan are "the very poster children for monogamy in the primate world," with a pattern of relationships that appeared to be "in the style of 1950s-era American television shows." Honey (which is the name of a gibbon I have met; see chapter four), I'm home!

However, gibbons are more like us in this emotionally charged social arena than previously imagined. Just as I teach in my anthropology class, the overwhelming norm in human societies is monogamy, but family flexibility is a feature of marriage and family in nearly all such societies. Not everyone is a single or a serial monogamist.

One clear reason why monogamy is the main model for gibbons lies in the area of sexual dimorphism, the differences in size between adult males and females. Unlike gorillas, orangutans and walruses, there is very little difference in gender size, even less than with humans. You have to look carefully in zoos to determine who the females and males are. It helps if they like to sunbathe, or just lie around.

Often writers talking about the size of a particular gibbon species will give one figure, without differentiating between the two sexes. Both researchers in the field and visitors to a zoo are hard-pressed to determine which gibbons are female and which are male simply by casual glancing. I know I often have a hard time in zoos I have visited. And the fact that gibbons are usually not clearly sexually dichromatic—each sex having its own distinct colour pattern—contributes to this recognition problem. The point here is that when males and females are similar in size, polygamy (technically *polygyny*–plurality of females) becomes less likely. Biologists doing field and comparative studies point to evolutionary and environmental reasons why this monogamous model may work well for a species. They sometimes speak of constraints of territory and resources. You can also read about the male mating strategy (reproductive success) and female strategy (prevention of infanticide, which unfortunately does happen with chimps and gorillas when a new male has successfully taken over a harem from a former alpha male).

Gibbon monogamy has been connected with singing strategies. Male or female solos can be thought of as warnings to outsiders that there is a strong male or female gibbon here, so don't come near if you are the same gender. Song duets between mates are often considered a way of re-inforcing pair bonding. If you sing together, you stay together (and if you are human, you annoy everyone else in the car).

There are exceptions to the monogamy or pair-bonding rule. This has been demonstrated in a 14-year study (1992–2006) of 250 social groups and seven solitary individuals of the white-handed gibbons of Khao Yai, Sumatra. One female, Andromeda, was the local record holder, with eight different sexual partners. She was in a galaxy all by herself.

WHAT INQUIRING STUDENTS WANT TO KNOW ABOUT GIBBONS

This book is written so that everyone from those ten or 11 years old to seniors can read it. Local grade six students in Bolton, Ontario, have been very helpful to me in the writing of this book. The following are questions asked me by grade six students I have spoken and listened to in visits to schools.

Q: Who first discovered gibbons?

A: Two kinds of answers can be given. The quick and narrow answer would be to look to the French in India in the second half of the eighteenth century, as they brought the word *gibbon* to the languages and knowledge base of Europe. India is the home of the Hoolock gibbons, *hoolock* being a local word for the ape. But the French no more discovered gibbons than Christopher Columbus discovered the Americas. They just further global-ized knowledge of an animal already known for thousands of years to non-Europeans. It might be fair to say the ancestors of most of the humans alive today knew about gibbons for thousands of years—the people whose descendants now live in China, India, Bangladesh, Myanmar, Thailand, Vietnam, Malaysia and Indonesia. The early writers in those traditions are close to invisible to Western scholarship, and certainly to students and many teachers in Western schools at all levels.

The first white man to encounter gibbons may have been Marco Polo (c.1254–1324), although if he did meet gibbons, they weren't living ones. The Italian explorer, who travelled along the silk route to go deep into southeastern Asia, wrote in the third book of his voyages about the bizarre practice of making *fake pygmies*, which he came across on the Indonesian island of Sumatra:

> I may tell you moreover that when people bring home pygmies which they allege to come from India, 'tis all a lie and a cheat. For those little men, as they call them, are manufactured on this Island, and I will tell you how. You see there is on the Island a kind of monkey which is very small, and has a face just like a man's. They take these, and pluck out all the hair except the hair of the beard and on the breast, and then they dry them and stuff them and daub them with saffron and other things until they look like men. But you see it is all a cheat; for nowhere in India nor anywhere else in the world were there ever men seen so small as these pretended pygmies.

Were these "pretended pygmies" actually gibbons? It is hard to say. There is recent speculation among some scientists that Marco Polo was referring to *Homo floresiensis* (nicknamed "the Hobbit" by some writers), which is presently confounding and confusing anthropologists with its short size (roughly one metre tall) and recent presence (within the last 17,000 years). It was discovered on the small Indonesian island of Flores, and it is debated whether or not the single well-known specimen was a different species from us. However, I believe that what Marco Polo saw were gibbons. In chapter five, I will present evidence as to why I think that might be.

Q: Where does the name *gibbon* come from, and what does it mean?

A: There is a bit of mystery here. We don't really know. We know that the word first appeared in print in 1766 in the writings of Georges-Louis Leclerc Comte de Buffon (1707–1788), in his *Nomenclature of the Apes*, part of the fourteenth volume of his *Histoire Naturelle*. It is uncertain how he came up with the term "gibbon." Some have theorized it came from a French and Old English term related to cats, *gib*. This seems a bit of a stretch (a good phrase to use when speaking about gibbons), although gibbons are the weight of a big housecat. There is another unsubstantiated hypothesis that Buffon named the ape after the English historian Edward Gibbon (1737–1794), who, like Buffon, frequented the salon of Madame Suzanne Necke. There may have been some jealousy between the two men. If such was the case, I am glad that they were called "gibbons" and not "buffons."

Buffon had actually seen a young male gibbon, and included a description in his biological writings published in 1785:

> The Gibbon keeps himself always erect, even when he walks on four feet; because his arms are as long as both his body and legs. . . . [H]e is distinguished from the other apes by the prodigious length of his arms. . . . His face is flat . . . and pretty similar to that of man. After the orang-outang and the pigmy [chimpanzee], the gibbon would make the nearest approach to the human figure, if he was not deformed by the excessive length of his arms; for, in a state of nature, man would likewise have a strange aspect. The hair would form round his countenance [i.e., face] a circle similar to that which surrounded the fact of the gibbon.

Now from a gibbon's point of view, we are deformed by the excessive shortness of our arms and length of our legs. And I have a gibbon-like "strange aspect" to my face, with my beard, long hair, and bald top of the head. Another hypothesis holds that the name *gibbon* came back to Europe from India, reputedly through Joseph François Dupleix, who was the French Governor-General in India from 1742 to 1754.

The first scientific name for gibbons was coined by the master classifier, Karl Linnaeus, who in 1771 referred to white-handed gibbons (now known as *Hylobates lar*), and to gibbons generally as *Homo lar*. Gibbons, like chimps, were put into the same genus as humans or *Homo sapiens*. Within a short time they would be downgraded to *Simia* as a genus (as were chimps). After that gibbons were called more specifically *Hylobates*.

Q: Where are gibbons?

The obvious answer to the question of "Where are gibbons?" would be "some 100 feet in the trees." More seriously, gibbons live in the Indian subcontinent in Bangladesh and the northeastern states of India. They also live in southern parts of China, but not across the wide range they used to have, and perhaps, soon, not at all outside of zoos. Gibbons live in the southeastern Asian countries of Cambodia, Laos, Myanmar, Thailand and Vietnam. Indonesia, a large country made up of large and small islands (Borneo, Java and Sumatra come to mind), has a good number of gibbon species. So does the neighbouring large country also made up of large and small islands (plus a peninsula), Malaysia.

Q: What do gibbons eat?

A: One of the questions I'm most often asked by students when lecturing at primary schools is: What do gibbons eat? What is their food? Are they herbivores, carnivores or omnivores? The gibbon is, in fact, a *frugivore*, a fruit eater, fruit being the main part of the gibbon diet, with figs especially favoured. Gibbons, however, also eat shoots, leaves, bugs, and the occasional bird's eggs. In Thad Bartlett's thorough accounting of the food eaten by the white-handed gibbons he studied, he reckoned that fruit made up about two-thirds of the gibbons' annual diet (non-fig fruit, 46.7% and figs 18.8%, for a total of 65.5%), with the remainder made up of leaves (22.3%), insects (8.7%), vine shoots (2.2%), and flowers (1.3%). Bartlett also noted gibbons ate parts of 101 different species of plant. Compare that with the number of different plants that you eat.

In chapter five you will encounter Mary, the Müller's gibbon who lives in a zoo in Sydney, Australia. Here is an example of her daily diet at one period of her life:

Fruit	Vegetables
1 apple	1 carrot
2 bananas	1 celery stick
½ orange	¼ chili pepper
½ pear	1 shallot
A little bit of pineapple	¼ sweet potato

Q: How do gibbons drink?

A: I am tempted to answer this with the words "with great difficulty," but that is only how it might seem to a human. How a gibbon drinks is fascinating, and would be interesting to watch. My reading suggests to me that it is a process unique to gibbons. C. R. Carpenter, the first researcher to engage in a thorough scientific study of gibbons, composed a very detailed description of the process as practised by the white-handed gibbons of his study:

> Where there is a collection of water, wild gibbons characteristically close their fingers, dip the hand into the water and then suck the moisture from the hairs of the back of their hand and

knuckles. Usually the hand is dipped into the water and then brought quickly above the mouth as the head is thrown backward. Thus the collected drops of water both drip into and are sucked into the mouth. . . . Some gibbons with considerable delicacy dip only the hairs of the back of the hand into the water, while others plunge the entire hand in and collect some water in their poorly formed fist.

Sometimes gibbons even rub their hairy hands on especially wet leaves. Given how dense their fur is, this is a productive strategy, because the thick hair acts like a sponge. They occasionally get their water from hollow places in trees after a rain. They also have been known to suspend themselves from a low branch by their feet and dip their hands into a water source. With these methods, they don't have to touch the ground, where predators become more of a threat. They tend not to bathe—it's too dangerous.

Q: Can gibbons swim?

A: They can't. That is one reason why a moat is used as a kind of barrier for gibbons (and other hominoids) in compounds in zoos (although in chapter five you'll find an example of a moat not exactly working). Carpenter tested whether gibbons could swim across rivers. As useful as many of the results of his studies were, there is a kind of cold and creepy lack of emotional attachment evident in his writing that reflects the stereotype of the heartless scientist of the 1930s (a period in which a good number of scientists condoned the eugenic sexual sterilization of those humans thought to be inferior to the norm):

> On May 18, 1937 a fully adult female gibbon was repeatedly tested for swimming ability in a calm pool of water near my camp at Doi Dao. Taking the ape by the hand, I gently [?] threw her about six feet from the bank into water several feet deep [probably over her head]. The responses of the animal consisted of throwing back and raising its head, general struggling movements, threshing about and uncoordinated movements of legs and arms [i.e., panicking]. The thick long wool rapidly became water soaked and in less than a minute, on three successive trials, she began to sink. I pulled her ashore with the light cord which was tied around her hips. I believe that with this particular type of ape, wide waterways would be barriers to geographical dispersion.

Q: What colour are gibbons?

A: Their colours range from black to silver to buff/blond. There are no bright colours such as orangutan orange. Although no species of gibbon is completely white, faces tend to have some white on them, while hands and feet sometimes do. It seems to me that the default colour is black, particular the males of whatever species.

Q: How long do gibbons live?

A: This is a difficult question to answer. I have noticed, for example, that website entries on white-cheeked gibbons routinely say that their lifespan in the wild is 28 years. One of my favourite teacherly questions is "How do you know that?" How would scientists know how long a white-cheeked gibbon lives in the wild? They would have to tag them when they are infants, which would be very difficult to do, more difficult than with geese, whales or deer or wolves, which are tranquillized and then tagged for research purposes. I would think that shooting a gibbon with a tranquillizer gun would make it fall fast and hard—not to be advised. If they did not do that, how would they know how old a wild gibbon was at death? My feeling is that they don't know. Gibbons are not trees. They don't grow rings every year.

We know that gibbons can live in zoos into their fifties. They are safer there, as there are no predators. However, they do not get to swing as far and as often. It can be a good life in the compound, especially one that is enriched with swings, ropes and other things to swing from, and it may add years to their lifespan.

Q: Are gibbons dangerous?

A: I have often been asked by grade six students if gibbons can be dangerous. This is an important question for those who think that they might make good pets. When young, they are as cute and cuddly as you could want a pet to be. I know when my wife Angie and I first met with Penelope at the Bowmanville Zoo, we would at that moment gladly have taken her home. There was no way in which she could harm us. But like baby raccoons (which I wanted to have as a child), and baby foxes, gibbons can become quite dangerous when they get older, especially when their long canines grow in. And both males and females have long canines. Penelope has long canines now.

In Jeanne Ann Vanderhoef's 1996 publication *Gibbons in the Family*, she illustrates what can happen when gibbons grow up:

> One afternoon, in the fall of 1961, Lee [Jeanne Ann's young daughter] and I brought the gibbons in from outside in time for their supper. They lived with us for five years by then and the routine was well-established. Lee was taking off Pogo's belt and apparently caught a little of his fur. He squeaked; Penny tore away from me and before I even thought to grab her, she attacked Lee and tore Lee's ear lobe. Fortunately, it healed well, but I knew then that something had to be done before we had a greater tragedy.

She called the director of the National Zoo in Washington (her husband was high up in the military establishment), and asked about whether the gibbons could have their canines removed. She received the following response. While the language used is a little archaic and also a bit insulting to gibbons—for example, they don't have "little brains"; their brains are relatively large for their body size—the message is important:

> Please, Mrs. Vanderhoef, find a zoo that will accept them while you still have a face without scars. . . . Gibbons are wild animals and, as such, are subject to what we call "red-outs." Now that Penny has reached adolescence and Pogo is almost there, if they become upset or frightened, their little brains will explode in frenzy and—for long enough to do considerable damage—they won't know what they're doing. Penny will be terribly contrite when her mind clears, but the damage will have been done.

After one of the gibbons attacked one of the servants, biting her rather savagely in the leg, the Vanderhoefs arranged to have their beloved pets housed in the Cleveland Zoo.

Mrs. Vanderhoef later wanted to visit her former pets, but she was worried they might get upset by seeing her. The director of the zoo responded by saying, "Oh, don't worry. They've been here a year and a half. They won't even remember you. I hope that doesn't hurt you, but that's the way animals are."

When Mrs. Vanderhoef arrived at the gibbons' compound, Penny was eating a banana, and Pogo was eating an orange:

When Pogo's bright eyes scanning the crowd met mine, the orange dropped.

"Eeeee!" he shrieked. "Eeeee! Eeeee!" He swung down and ran to the window. Penny looked out, saw me, threw away the banana and rushed with Pogo across the floor. . . . Drawn, as if by magnet, I pushed my way to the window. We met, the glass a barrier between my yearning arms and the furry ones so anxious to twine around my neck.

I pushed so hard trying to reach through, my hands on the glass must have left indelible prints. Penny and Pogo's tiny hands pushed equally as hard from the other side.

They remembered her.

Q: What are the main predators of gibbons?

A: The short answer is humans, big cats, big snake, big birds, and maybe in the future big dogs. See chapter six for a more complete answer.

Q: At what age do the children leave the nest and go off on their own?

A: I find this an interesting question coming from an 11- or 12-year-old human. Generally speaking, young gibbons leave or are driven out a short time after they reach maturity, although this is not a hard and fast rule for all species. This should happen at or before the time they turn eight, when they are gibbon adults. See chapters three and four in the discussions on siamangs for a look at how this happens.

Speaking of nests, there were several student questions about nests, sleeping arrangements (i.e., did everyone sleep in the same tree, did they change the trees in which they slept?), and whether gibbons slept in the day or night. Alone among the apes, gibbons do not make nests. They do, around dusk, find a tall tree above the canopy. For Western hoolocks (a gibbon found in India, Bangladesh and Myanmar), the average height of their lodging, roosting or sleeping trees is ten to 30 metres (i.e., up to some 100 feet or more in the air), and they snuggle into the most comfortable branch (always remembering not to roll over in their sleep). Family members, usually a father and mother and one to three children, do not all sleep in the same tree. A mother and infant might do so.

Q: Are gibbons smart?

A: Are gibbons smart—are they intelligent? And is their intelligence invisible (to return to a major theme of this book) to the human eye, a kind of "swing intelligence" that humans don't see as they are not in the trees to truly appreciate what the gibbons are doing there? These are difficult questions to answer. As a long-time fan of evolutionary biologist Stephen J. Gould, particularly his book *The Mismeasure of Man*, I'm a big believer that there is no one intelligence that you can measure on a scale with a single number. Part of this involves becoming aware that humans have different intelligences and different intelligence levels, and so do non-humans. We (humans and non-humans) do not all excel in the same areas. Both of my dogs have a much higher smell intelligence than I do (notice I did not say that they smell better than I do, because they don't).

Gibbons develop certain behaviours more rapidly than we do. In a study of two young male black-handed gibbons—brothers—it was noted that they attempted crawling at 13 weeks, slower than Japanese macaques (one week) and chimpanzees (eight weeks), but sooner than humans (36 weeks), and with similar results for reaching by hand: seven weeks for one brother, eight weeks for the other, one week in Japanese macaques, 14 weeks for chimps, and humans lagging behind at 20 weeks. In 2008, An-nica Poyas and Thad Q. Bartlett published a study of infant development of a male captive white-cheeked gibbon (*Nomascus leucogenys*) named Gibson living in the San Antonio Zoo and found that by the thirtieth week the little one was walking on two feet. I know that I (along with my species generally) was not bipedal that early in life.

But these are unfair tests for humans. During the first year our brains are still forming, not yet reaching full size or development. We are not yet playing with a full head. That is not true of the other primates. My point is that tests for one species might not be reasonable points of comparison for others.

Let's ask the gibbon intelligence question differently, then. Is being like us necessarily a sign of gibbon intelligence? Or is their "best" intelligence shown in areas that differ from our "best" areas? Does performing in human-structured tests, with expected human-like responses being the right answer, indicate how smart they truly are? I know that these are loaded questions, but I feel that too often they have been loaded on the other side, the negative side. It is much the same situation as when people ask me, as they invariably seem to do, "Can your parrots talk?"—as if par-rots could do nothing more intelligent than parrot my human sounds and not have different meanings of their own embedded in their many com-munications, sounds that require some sharp human thinking skills to interpret. I sometimes wonder whether other parrots ask ours, "Do your humans understand our language?"

One human-set test of intelligence that it was long thought that only we passed was the tool-use test. Humans (or, as it was usually put in the early days of anthropology, *men*) are tool users. That was thought to be one of the key things that separated us from the animals.

Then the bad news for human exclusivity came from the Jane Goodall chimpanzee camp. Chimps peel sticks, put them in the top holes of termite hills, wait for the termites to crawl onto the sticks, and then withdraw the sticks covered with crawling food, which they lick up. Other chimps break hard-to-crack nuts by using well-chosen rocks both as anvils and hammers. The little ones watch and learn the culture that their troop has that other troops don't, and consequently don't learn.

Orangutans have demonstrated their ingenuity in preparing sticks of the right length to help them gain access to the soft juicy part of spiny fruits. They use leaves as gloves and as sponges to draw liquid from. And a few gorillas have been recorded as preparing and saving sticks of a particular length to test the swampland for deep water as they cross over. And recently, too, have come all the reports of what the New Caledonian crows can do. And it seemed strange to me that the sea otters using stones on their chests to break shellfish as they float on their backs for a long time wasn't considered as tool use

Egwene (1997–2010), a very intelligent border collie still dear to our hearts although she is now physically gone, could make a fetching stick when there weren't any to be found in a small park near where we live. Once she ripped a maple root up from the ground, separating it from the rest of the tree, picked it up and dropped it at my feet. Message received, girl. More recently, Stanee, our female green-cheeked conure (a long-tailed small parrot), before she paired up with Louie, used to pick up a plastic straw and then, standing on one talon, she would scratch the back of her neck where Louie now preens her. Our Quaker parrots, Finn and Quigley, have been known to deliberately amplify their vocal performances by sticking their heads into coffee cups or paper towel tubes when laughing like a human.

So, do gibbons use tools? Gibbons are at a slight disadvantage in tool manipulating because of the fact that their thumbs are more separate and differently separated from their other fingers than is the case with other apes, including us. It is part of their being adapted primarily to swinging through the trees. I first saw the "awkwardness" of gibbon hand use when

I observed a young white-handed gibbon (the often-mentioned Penelope, whom you will get to know better in chapter four) grab a piece of banana by pressing it with her thumb against the palm of her hand instead of against her index or third finger as we would do. That looked awkward to me.

However, primatologist Thomas Geissmann demonstrated a gibbon's capacity for tool use in his 2009 article, "Door slamming: Tool-use by a captive white-handed gibbon (*Hylobates lar*)." In this interesting article, Geissmann talks about how a female white-handed gibbon would slam open the sliding door of her wooden sleeping box as a way of adding a per-cussive climax to her "great call," the long song performance that female gibbons engage in. For me, this is stronger evidence of gibbons' tool-using capacity than psychologists having hoolocks use a rake to obtain or lose food (a test in which they performed "moderately better" than chimps or capuchin monkeys) or presenting gibbons with string-pulling problems. In this case, the tool use was invented by a white-handed gibbon without the situation being contrived by humans.

Q: What kind of contests do gibbons play?
A: One of the grade six students asked, "What kind of contests do they play?" This is another question that is more interesting than it sounds at first. The interest stems from the fact that gibbons generally do not play with other gibbons their own age. Gibbons typically live in nuclear family groups, and at certain stages they may play with mom, even dad (es-pecially siamang children), and with older and younger siblings. But much of their play is alone, swinging, hanging alone, playing with whatever they find in the trees. There are no *contests* as such between gibbons of the same age. They have to settle for individual excellence.

Q: What is a group of gibbons called?
A: A swing set. Okay, that's just a joke. More seriously, I know of no term used for a group other than "family." A nuclear family, with one to three children, is the prevalent pattern. Gibbons do not travel in packs, herds, schools, troops or even gangs. The nuclear family unit is basic.

Q: If the girl and boy dislike each other, how do they mate?
A: This is an interesting question from an 11- or 12-year-old, just on the cusp of adolescence and those raging hormonal teenage years. Sometimes when zoos transport a gibbon to be the mate of a "single" gibbon at an-

other zoo, the arranged relationship does not work. Gibbons, like humans (and in my experience, also parrots), find some potential mates easier to get along with than others, and are sometimes not shy in expressing their dislike of their intended mates. Drugs have been used to de-stress their first encounters. Chapters four and five will present some examples of this potentially stressful situation. In the wild I imagine mate-choosing is a matter of opportunity and compatibility, a lot like humans "in the wild."

Q: Can gibbons be right-handed or left-handed?

A: This is my question. Tony Whitten answered this question in part with the following description of two Kloss's gibbons, Katy and Sam:

> By noting which hand she used for wiping up ants and for picking fruit, I was able to discover that Katy was noticeably right-handed. Conversely, Sam was left-handed and would position himself on a bough so that he could use his left hand for delicate jobs, and his right for holding on.

The Show So Far

So now you know the basics of what gibbons are like. They are monogamous, singing, swinging, nuclear-family living, non-swimming, fruit-eating, intelligent, long-armed small apes (therefore having no tails). They live in the tall trees in south, southeast and east Asia. And they are fascinating creatures. They are certainly worth reading a few more chapters about.

CHAPTER THREE

Gibbon Species

T his is probably the most scientific chapter in the book. So to keep you interested, I want to entice you by mentioning some of the stories you will find in these pages. You will read the sad story about a gibbon forced to fight for his life in staged death-matches. You will encounter a tale (not a tail!) of a gibbon named after a child-sacrificing god. You will be told a scandalous story about a woman who had an affair with a gibbon (it is only a myth). And for a "fun fact," you will learn how gibbon poop can be useful (but not around the house), and much, much more. Science can be interesting. It's all in the delivery.

But first here's a quiz. You should be able to answer these questions by the time that you have finished this chapter (and I'll include a summary of the answers at the end of the chapter, too):

1. How many genera (plural of genus) of gibbons are there?

a. two

b. five

c. the last one died out six years ago

d. four.

2. How many species of gibbon are there?

a. 10

b. 12

c. 17

d. I think I will wait until the next major research report comes out.

3. What species of gibbon are you most likely to see in a zoo in North America?

a. *H. lar* or white handed gibbons

b. *N. hainanus* or Hainan black-crested gibbons

c. None, as they are invisible.

4. What genus of gibbon is the largest in size?

a. *Hylobates agilis*

b. Siamangs

c. *Hylobates pileatus.*

Now on to the answers.

How Many Species of Gibbons Are There?

That's a good question to ask, and a hard one to answer. Trying to find a consistent number for how many recognized species of gibbons exist can be confusing. Just about every book or article that you read presents a different number. Over the past 30 years it has been reported that there are nine, 11, 12, 13, 14, 15 and 16 different species of gibbons. Generally speaking, the newer the work that you read, the larger the number of gibbon species to which it refers. Four years ago, in an early draft of this book, I wrote: "For our purposes here, I will say that there are 16 species. There is a good chance that might be right. But I could be wrong."

I *was* wrong, and should have known better. There are now thought to be 17 species. The newest species to be identified is the northern buffed-cheeked gibbon, which was identified about the same time that I wrote the three sentences quoted above. Welcome to the growing club, northern buffed-cheeked gibbon. We hope to keep seeing you for a long time.

To add to the confusion, at least for an old anthropology teacher such as myself, is the fact that the big guys, the siamangs (weighing over 20 pounds), are now more closely linked with other gibbons in the scientific literature than they were in the past. I got very used to referring to "gibbons and siamangs" in the classroom. That distinction was set up in 1933 by early primatologist Adolph Schultz. It lasted until fairly recently. Maybe I should have my early students recalled so that this new piece of information can be recorded in a chip to be embedded in their brains.

You can readily see why the number of species keeps increasing. In many of the areas of Southeast Asia in which they live, gibbons are not very accessible for researchers to study. They are small and really good at hiding. They move fast, and do so high in the trees far from human sight. And those trees are situated in places that are not very accessible to pedestrian, not-brachiating human researchers. Research helicopters are way too expensive. And it would be very difficult to set up stationary cameras anywhere near where gibbons sleep, travel or eat.

The ground below the gibbons is an often swampy, bug and pest-infested territory tough on primatologists trying to get close to the subjects of their study. That is one reason why primatologists trying to get gibbon counts for population censuses often do so by identifying individual groups by their songs and not by their physical appearance. Gibbons in the wild are much easier to hear than they are to see. But, unfortunately, while songs can be species-distinctive, there is some overlap in gibbon singing. The songs of different species can be quite similar, much like pop songs in any given year.

Reading the following passage from Thad Bartlett's excellent work on white-handed gibbons, *The Gibbons of Khao Yai: Seasonal Variation in Behavior and Ecology* (2009), should give you a good sense of how determined someone has to be to do gibbon field research, and how difficult it would be to make distinctions between species in the field (realistically, "in the tall trees" would be a more apt term):

> We had been walking for a few hours without a glimpse of gibbons, long enough that I had already started to wonder if I would have to wait another day, or longer, to finally see the animals I proposed to study for the coming year. My anxiety was temporarily eased as we crossed over a small ravine, and Warren pointed up into the crown of an unimaginably large tree. It was a sprawling Ficus [fig tree] that soared over a hundred feet in the air, and high overhead was a family of gibbons moving through the distant branches. Certainly it was a climactic moment, but even though I felt a burst of exhilaration, it was quickly followed by a sense of alarm. I was shocked by how hard it was to see the animals, which compared to their surroundings looked more like squirrels than apes, and I began to wonder how I was ever going to follow them for a full day, let alone simultaneously collect behavioral data.

I'm glad that I did my short stint of fieldwork with gibbons in zoos. The height of their compounds allows for convenient human viewing. They are easy to spot, even without signs saying "This Way to the Gibbons," and even though they might be invisible to other zoo visitors. Once you get to know it, a gibbon face provides great clues as to what is hanging from a branch or pole above you. The long arms help, too.

The number of gibbon species recognized by scientists has increased for a number of reasons. Decades of research have created a much larger sampling of gibbons than before. Unfortunately, there has also been a reduction of gibbon habitat, which makes them easier to spot in some locations because they have to do some travelling on the ground and in shorter-than-safe trees. Thirdly, advances in genetics have enabled scientists to better distinguish between species. As access to gibbons (in the wild and in zoos and sanctuaries) has increased, and as genetic techniques (DNA identification) have advanced, the numbers of species has risen.

How Many Gibbon Genera Are There?

When a plant or an animal has a scientific name, that name has two parts: *genus* and *species*. You can remember this by keeping in mind that **gen**us is the **gen**eral term, referring to a group, and **speci**es is a **speci**fic term, referring to only one type. We humans, for example, are *Homo sapiens*, belonging to the genus *Homo* (meaning "man," like the French word *homme*) and the species *sapiens* (which means "thinking," although that is truer for some of us than for others). After you have named a plant or an animal once in something you are writing, you can shorten the genus down to the first letter, as in "*H. sapiens.*" This is very useful when you are writing about pre-humans known as Australopithecus!

The plural of genus is *genera*. As with species, the number of gibbon genera has increased over the decades. The number of gibbon genera currently identified is four. This is a number I would say will last a long time. It is based on chromosome count.

What is a chromosome? *Chromosomes* are bodies found in the nucleus of each cell. You should also know that chromosomes hang around in pairs, never alone. What does a chromosome look like? Pictures of chromosomes make me think of the Ents of *Lord of the Rings*, the walking trees, who came in to save the intrepid band of hobbits and their companions. Picture X's with long legs, and that gives you some sense of what a chromosome looks like. Different chromosomes are different sizes. In humans, chromosome two is huge by chromosome standards, though still tiny by everyday standards (after all, it has to fit within the cell nucleus).

Chromosomes were discovered when my grandfather John Charles Steckley was a small lad, in the late 19th century. They were called chromosomes because it was discovered that they held dye well (the Greek word *chromos* refers to colour). That enabled scientists with microscopes to see them fairly clearly, even though chromosomes are very, very small. But with early microscopes, scientists could not see them clearly enough, for they initially got the number of chromsomes possessed by humans wrong.

Fast forward to the time when I was a wee toddler walking awkwardly down the streets of northern Toronto in the early 1950s, parents watching closely as I was (and am) impulsive. Up until then, biology textbooks had informed us that humans have 24 pairs of chromosomes, the same number as the great apes (orangutans, gorillas, chimpanzees and bonobos, which were formerly called pygmy chimps). It was then discovered that humans in fact have 23 pairs. The old figure of 24 was the result of the fact that one of our chromosomes (chromosome two, mentioned above) is made up of two chimpanzee chromosomes mashed together into one very big chromosome. To the other chromosomes that twosome would look like the Godzilla of the chromosomes.

Each chromosome is made up of a single molecule of DNA—the molecule that carries the genetic code—as well as proteins (one of the other building blocks of life). Each DNA molecule is wound around the proteins in the chromosome in such a way that it can be made compact enough to fit into the nucleus of the cell. If you could stretch that DNA molecule out straight, it would be several centimetres long!

Within the DNA molecule are smaller units called "nucleotide bases." Strings of nucleotide bases make up units called "genes," which either alone or in combination with other genes determine specific properties that we inherit from our parents—everything from eye colour to the size of our noses.

Gibbons differ from the other apes and even among themselves when it comes to chromosome number. The latter fact still boggles my mind. Usually differences in chromosome count imply huge physical differences. To me this fact suggests that gibbon genera were separated a long, long time ago.

Gibbons are split into four genera, differing by as many as 14 in the number of chromosomes. Again, that is just amazing. That seems like a lot of difference to me. The four genera are *Hylobates, Hoolock, Nomascus* and *Symphalangus* (the siamangs, formerly considered more distinct from other gibbons than they are today). The first genus has 44 chromosomes (22 pairs), the second has 38 (19 pairs), the third 52 (26 pairs) and the last 50 (25 pairs). And yet all these gibbons look quite similar.

Even the current set of genera names is new. *Hoolock* was named as a genus as recently as 2006. Biology, like other sciences, is always changing, benefitting from recent research, particularly of the genetic variety. Your high school biology textbook got out-of-date quite quickly.

Gibbons' Chromosome Count

Genus	Chromosome Count
Hylobates	44
Hoolock	38
Nomascus	52
Symphalangus	50

Just to give you a sense of how gibbons' chromosome counts match up with those of other mammals, here is a list of some Canadian mammals chosen at random with their accompanying chromosome count.

Selected Mammals' Chromosome Count

Genus	Chromosome Count
Coyotes, dogs and wolves	78
Black bears and polar bears	74
White-tailed deer	70
American bison, cows	60
Humans	46
Beavers, mice, cats and pigs	38
Porcupines and red foxes	34

Characteristics Distinguishing Species within Gibbon Genera

How do you distinguish between species within a particular genus? One fairly clear way (in some cases) is *pelage*, which is a fancy term meaning fur colouring and patterning. I have facial pelage (a beard) that has whitened over the years, while my top-of-the-head pelage has completely disappeared. Another way involves vocalizations or songs. Sure, individuals differ in their songs and as a result can be identified by people who have spent serious time listening to them. And some gibbons can learn the songs of other species (witness Lenny and Holly in the next chapter learning from recordings). However, gibbons' songs have for the most part been demonstrated to be genetically programmed. This suggests that in a number of circumstances, a different song or set of songs can identify a different species or subspecies. Individuals do develop variations on a theme, kind of like jazz musicians. Songs can also be used in some limited cases to demonstrate relationships between different species. There are two gibbon species (Moloch gibbons and Kloss's gibbons) who do not sing duets between pairs. I guess they sing alone in a rain shower. This similarity in singing patterns suggested a connection between the two gibbon species that later genetic study supported.

The following table presents all of the genera and species of gibbons, as the naming situation stood late in the year 2014.

Genera and Species of Gibbons

Genus	Species	Common Names
Hylobates	lar	White-handed or common
	agilis	Agile or black-handed
	albibarbis	White-bearded
	muelleri	Müller's or grey
	moloch	Silvery
	pileatus	Pileated or capped
	klossi	Kloss's or Mentawi
Hoolock	hoolock	Western hoolock
	leuconedys	Eastern hoolock
Symphalangus	syndactylus	Siamangs
Nomascus	anamensis	Northern buffed-cheeked
	concolor	Concolor or black-crested
	nasutus	Eastern black-crested
	hainanus	Hainan
	leucogenys	Northern white-cheeked
	siki	Southern white-cheeked
	gabriellae	Yellow-cheeked or golden-cheeked

The Hylobates Species
HYLOBATES LAR: THE WHITE-HANDED GIBBON
You may have noticed in earlier chapters that studies I have referred to typically relate to white-handed gibbons. *Hylobates lar* also seems espe-

cially favoured as the gibbon of choice in zoos in North America. I sometimes refer to them as default gibbons. Alan Mootnik in 1984 wrote that of the 557 gibbons then in zoos in Canada and U.S., 342 were *H. lar*, or 61.4% of the North American zoo gibbon population. All of the six zoos that Angie and I visited in Southern Ontario have white-handed gibbons; only two of them have other gibbon species as well. My own mental image of a gibbon is of a white-handed gibbon. And Penelope, our cover girl, is a *Hylobates lar*.

The backs of the hands of *H. lar* are not the only parts that are white. Their face has a white ring around their big dark eyes, nose and mouth. Their feet are white, too. The rest of their colouring varies from an ash-blond, to a reddish buff, to a dark brown, to black. These colours are not specific or confined to one gender. You have to look carefully to determine what sex a white-handed gibbon is. But don't stare.

They are mid-sized for a gibbon, weighing 4.5 to 6 kilograms or 9.9 to 13.2 pounds as adults, both males and females. Adult males typically weigh about one pound more than the females do, but that is not something that you can spot when you see gibbons in a zoo.

White-handed gibbons were the earliest of the family to be classified specifically as gibbons and have been historically the most often studied of all the gibbon species. However, their current status as the most prominently represented gibbon in the literature was not always secure. In William Jardine's work about primates, published in 1866, they were barely even mentioned, unlike the siamang, the hoolock and the agile gibbon, which were described at great length.

The *lar* part of the same came from early Swedish biologist Carl Linnaeus. I don't know where he got the name—his long-favoured and long-armed Swedish uncle perhaps, Uncle Lars (joke!). In 1771, Linnaeus referred to the species (and to gibbons generally) as *Homo lar*. Along with chimps, Linnaeus put gibbons in the same genus as *Homo sapiens* or humans. That shared status did not last long. We cannot have other apes in our genus.

White-handed gibbons have a wide geographic range, which extends from southern   through southeast Asia. In the wild they are found in Myanmar (Burma), Thailand, Malaysia, and Indonesia, and formerly in the south of China.

The first major scientific study of gibbons was engaged in by Clarence Ray Carpenter (1905–1975). Carpenter was a pioneer in the field study of gibbons. He did his work long before the now more famous ape studies engaged in by Jane Goodall, Dian Fossey and Biruté Galdikas. Much of what is known about white-handed gibbons, and about gibbons generally, comes from Carpenter's classic study, first published in 1940. It was reprinted in a collection of his work in 1964.

In 1937, as part of the Asiatic Primate Expedition, Carpenter went to study *H. lar* in Northern Thailand. From March 27 to June 18, he observed extensively, engaged in trudging *follows* (following a group) through the jungle and in the process recording the vocalizations of 20 different gibbon social groups. His innovative methods were copied by those who followed him (and the gibbons) in gibbon study. Fortunately, not later copied were his use of old and somewhat heartless methods, the kill-collecting and skinning of many of the subjects of his study. I really don't know how he could have done that after spending so much time with them. I certainly could not do it.

He noted that the canine teeth of males and females were of roughly the same length, something that significantly distinguishes gibbons from the great apes and monkeys. With those primates, the larger male canines present a threat to predators and to competitors. Even male humans have slightly longer canines on average than female humans do. I guess that makes them more likely to be cast as vampires in the movies.

Measurements taken during the expedition by Adolph Schultz allowed the following distinctions to be drawn concerning lower limb (leg) and upper limb (arm) length relative to the trunk or body. A figure of 100 percent indicates that the two features are the same size. Note that of the primates compared, we humans have the longest legs relative to the trunks of our bodies, and *H. lar* has the longest arms relative to their bodies. Monkeys display the smallest figures in both categories. If a primate had the relative leg length of a human and the relative arm length of a gibbon, that primate would look a lot like a spider with half the usual number of legs (or perhaps like an NBA basketball player with an extremely short trunk—not trun<u>ks</u>).

	Hylobates lar	Monkeys	Great Apes
Lower limb / Trunk height	147%	96%	112%–131%
Upper limb / Trunk height	238%	107%	154%–184%

Schultz also remarked on the differences in hair density: 2,035 hairs per square centimeter on the middle of the scalp, as compared to 910 in Old World (Africa and Asia) monkeys and 307 in great apes. That's hair like a sponge. Remember how they drink water? Recall that they do not swim.

LO

One personal gibbon face emerges in Carpenter's generally impersonal description of his *H. lar* study subjects. I think he actually liked her. Her name was Lo. Carpenter referred to gibbons in the wild by a letter for their group and a number for them individually, very scientifically neutral. This was not so with Lo. She was a female, between 3½ and four years old, who walked in a more accomplished bipedal way, rarely touching her hands to the ground, than did the other captive gibbons Carpenter reported on. Carpenter noted that this was a skill that she had improved on during her first month in their study camp. Practice might not always make perfect, but it does show how gibbon toddlers, like human ones, can improve their walking skills the more they travel on two legs. Can you imagine how much trouble gibbon toddlers could get into if they lived in a human home? They could reach high up into the cupboards, beyond the reach of their human counterparts. And then think of what they could do if they got up on a table over which there was hanging a chandelier.

A juvenile gibbon was placed in a cage with Lo and a young adult male called Franklin. While Franklin ignored the juvenile, Lo approached the young one repeatedly in a relatively easygoing way, making no moves to touch the juvenile. Carpenter wrote:

> It seemed obvious to me, though it didn't seem apparent to the young gibbon, that "Lo" was trying to be friendly. When at last "Lo" was allowed to come close, she sat down and gently folded the young one in her arms. After that it was never afraid of "Lo" again and "Lo" was its special protector for several months against "Franklin's" attempts at rough play.

Lo had broken through the scientist shell that Carpenter covered himself in. She was a person.

THE WHITE-HANDED GIBBONS OF KHAO YAI

Carrying on the scholarly tradition of scientific work on white-handed gibbons, but with the added qualifier that "no gibbons were harmed in the production of this work," is Thad Q. Bartlett's recent *The Gibbons of Khao Yai: Seasonal Variation in Behavior and Ecology* (2009).

Khao Yai ("Big Mountain") National Park, established in 1962, is the oldest such park in Thailand. In a country in which the percentage of forested land has dropped from 60% to less than 15%, protected spaces such as this national park are vital to gibbons' survival.

Included among Bartlett's carefully recorded technical findings are some interesting statements concerning how the white-handed gibbons that he studied spent their time each day. First I should note how life-stages are categorized in this type of research:

Infants	Birth to 2 years
Juvenile	2 to 5 years
Adolescent	5 to 8 years
Adult	8+ years

The term *sub-adult* is also used sometimes. Sub-adults are generally of the same age as young adults. They just haven't mated and established a home territory. They are in that sense a bit like humans in their twenties in Canada who still live in their parents' homes (we have a male human sub-adult living in our home now).

Here's how the two groups of gibbons Bartlett studied divided up their time. I have added to this chart the ones who have the highest and lowest percentage scores.

Activity	Percentage	Highest	Percentage	Lowest	Percentage
Feeding	32.6%	Juvenile	34.6%	Adult male	28.9%
Resting	26.2%	Adult male	33.1%	Juvenile	18.7%
Travelling	24.2%	Juvenile	31.1%	Adult male	18.5%
Social Activities	11.3%	Juvenile	13.7%	Adult female	9.3%
Vocalizing	4.0%	Adolescent	5.7%	Juvenile	1.2%
Intergroup Encounters	1.9%	Adult male	3.6%	Juvenile	0.6%

So, the juveniles feed, socialize and travel the most, rest and vocalize the least. Imagine spending over one-third of your day eating! I like the idea. Juvenile socializing is mostly play. They do relatively little grooming of others.

Dad rests a lot, but he is saving his strength to take care of intergroup encounters and, presumably, potential conflicts (at least, that's his story and he is sticking to it). Surprisingly, he spends the least time feeding (maybe he gibbons down his fruit quickly), and travels the least (it cuts down on his resting time). He does, however, groom more than the others do. This is something that I noted with Willy, Lilly and Chilly in our first visit to the Elmvale Zoo (discussed in the next chapter). Willy did most of the grooming.

Adolescents vocalize the most. Imagine if gibbons had cell phones. I don't think that their relatively small and separated thumbs would be good for texting. It was also later noted by Bartlett that adolescents were on the receiving end of most of the aggressive behaviour. The aggression involved their being driven away by the parents from feeding or drinking once there is a younger child that needs to eat and drink. In later chapters you will read stories about this. While adult females don't show up often in this score sheet in terms of highest or lowest scores, apart from participating in social activities least, it should be pointed out that they do place first in leading the family to different places for various activities:

> . . . group movement appears to be directed by adult females, who determine the timing and direction of travel. This is evident in that group members tend to converge on the female's night tree at the beginning of the day and in that adult females are regularly the first to enter, and especially the first to exit, feeding trees.

HYLOBATES AGILIS

Early in the nineteenth century in England, there were various kinds of "baiting" activities, in which animals fought to the death in a ring or arena. People bet on who the winner would be. Dogs, bears and monkeys were often participants in these nasty blood sports. One such participant was a famous gibbon fighter that I suspect might have been a *Hylobates agilis*. He was described as having black hands and face, both *H. agilis* characteristics. The gibbon's name was Jacco Macacco. His fame was forced upon him in the deadly monkey-baiting fight pits. He weighed about 4.5 kilograms (or 10 pounds), and was put up against dogs that were permitted to weigh no more than 20 pounds (to keep the battle "sporting"). Bets ranged from £10 to £50 (that would amount to hundreds of dollars in today's Canadian money) that the dog could not last five minutes with Jacco

Macacco. Fourteen fights and 14 victories (killings) were recorded for the combative Jacco. He had early learned to pounce on the dog's neck with his long canines and not let go. His fifteenth fight was lethal for him, as his jaw was ripped off by a dog named Puss. Both combatants died. Not long afterwards, Britain passed its first legislation against cruelty to animals. I like to think that the death of Jacco Macacco might have been a factor in the creation and passing of this important legislation.

H. agilis gibbons, otherwise called black- or dark-handed or agile gibbons, live wild in Thailand, mainland and island Malaysia, and Indonesia. The males differ from the females very slightly in that the males are said to have white on their cheeks. I didn't see the distinction between Kingfisher (male) and Fufanu (female), two *H. agilis* that will be described in the next chapter.

The name "agile" is not particularly distinctive because, of course, every species of gibbon is agile. Still, when you read Jardine's description of their locomotion, you can see why this gibbon species was bound to receive the name:

> They are endowed with surprising agility, and their light form and slender-looking extremities hardly give an idea of the great muscularity which they must possess. If the extreme tree on the borders of a forest can be reached by them it will be in vain to pursue farther; they swing, leap, and, as it were throw themselves from one tree to another, clearing at time a space of forty feet, with rapidity which defies any pedestrian pursuer. When a slender branch can be grasped, the body is swung several times until sufficient impetus is gained, and they then dart off with the utmost apparent ease and grace.

There is currently a dispute over whether *H. agilis* is one species or two. Three variants or sub-species exist, a lowland and mountain variant, as well as a variant that lives in the southwestern part of the Indonesian island of Borneo. Some feel that this last variant should be called *H. albibarbis*, and is a distinct species (as I have considered it here). The last part of the name means "white beard" (*albi* as in **albi**no, and *barb* meaning "beard"), which is a common name often given to the variant. As a *Homo sapiens albibarbis*, or white-bearded human, I like the name.

HYLOBATES PILEATUS

Hylobates pileatus or pileated gibbons live in eastern Thailand, western Cambodia and southwestern Laos. They are the most sexually dichromatic species within the *Hylobates* genus. Males and females have different colouring, with males having black fur over most of their body and females having lighter shades—buffish or white/grey. Both sexes start out light-coloured, with the males acquiring their black colouring by about age 6½ years. Females make a quicker change, reaching their unique version of light colouring about two years earlier. The species name "pileated" or, Latinized, *pileatus*, stems from their head colouring. "Pileated" means "to have a cap or crest." Think of having a *pile* of something on your head. If, like me, you have parrots that like to land on your head like a pile of feathers, it shouldn't be too difficult to imagine. The pileated woodpecker, for example, common in North America, has a red crest on top of its head. The pileated gibbon has a white crown-like circle surrounding a dark skull. In females the circle can extend out to look something like a very fluffy tiara (or a slightly out-of-control bad-hair day). Pileated gibbons are sometimes called capped or crowned gibbons, another way of saying the same thing as pileated.

It was estimated that there might have been over two million pileated gibbons in Thailand in the 1960s. That number may be too high, but with deforestation, only 36,000 survived by 1975. Some contemporary estimates place their number in that country at only 12,000. Hunting, not just deforestation, is also having a negative impact on their population.

The pileated gibbons had a great champion in Alan Mootnick, until his death in 2011 the head of the Gibbon Conservation Center in California (the GCC; see chapter seven for more on the organization). The GCC has the only successful pileated gibbon breeding program in the Americas. Other good programs are in Europe (France, the United Kingdom and Switzerland) and in Asia (Japan and Thailand). In 2013, there were only 20 pileated gibbons in North America, half of which were at the GCC.

In 2001, Kanako, a female pileated gibbon, was born to JR, a 13-year-old female on breeding loan from the Gladys Porter Zoo in Brownsville, Texas. Her father, named Biruté after the orangutan specialist, was a 21-year-old born at the Phoenix Zoo. At the time they were the only breeding pair of their species in North America, with only seven other pairs in zoos in Europe and Asia. Kanako joined her elder brother Mateas, born at the GCC on September 1, 1995, and older sister Valentine, born there as well, on July 27, 1998.

Once Mateas became an adolescent, he was moved out of the compound shared with his parents and relocated to live with one of the adult females. You can imagine his parents saying to him, "Mateas, we have some bad news and some good news."

How many pileated gibbons are there? In 2001, Alan Mootnick estimated that there were 50,000 of the species: 10,000 in Thailand, 10,000 in Laos, and 30,000 in Cambodia. By 2009, his estimates had dropped by 40%, to a total population of 30,000. Conservation programs are definitely necessary to rescue this species.

HYLOBATES MUELLERI

Hylobates muelleri is otherwise known as Müller's, the Bornean or the grey gibbon. The second name owes its origin to the fact that this species of gibbon lives on most of the island of Borneo, leaving exclusive room in the southwest for the closely related moloch gibbons. Their pelage is generally grey or brown, with a white-coloured ring around the face. Occasionally, they have a black or dark cap, especially the Eastern Müller's gibbon sub-species. They do not show any fur colour differences between the sexes, but there are slight variations among the three subspecies, silvery, mouse-gray or a darker colour. In chapter five you will read about the gibbon that might be the most famous of her species, once featured in an article entitled "Mary, Mary, Wild and Hairy." She is wild in spirit, even though she lives in a compound in an Australian zoo. Not all wild gibbons live in the wild.

HYLOBATES MOLOCH

Hylobates moloch is another gibbon with a number of names. And its primary name has sinister connotations. In the Bible, Moloch is the god of the Canaanites and the Phoenicians, to whom children were sacrificed. *H. moloch* is also called the Javan gibbon (after the large island on which it lives), more descriptively the silvery gibbon (as their fur colour is a brilliant silvery-grey) or the white-browed gibbon, a name I would never use as a good number of gibbon species share that not particularly distinctive trait.

They were first named scientifically as *Simia moloch* by French naturalist and nature artist Jean-Baptiste Audebert (1759–1800) in 1798. The term *simia* is derived from a Latin term for ape. Why he saw a sacrifice-demanding god in these generally gentle creatures is beyond me. Maybe one attacked and bit him.

Their pelage (or fur colour) is sometimes described as bluish gray, with a darker gray cap on top, with white brows, a colour combination shared by males and females. Sometimes in adult females, the chest is partly charcoal-coloured. An easier way to determine the sex of a *H. moloch* is in his or her singing. The females are the dominant singers, with males vocalizing only occasionally. They are like students that walk the halls of my college in that way. And they do not sing in duets, again a lot like my students.

They are mid-sized gibbons, with the adult males weighing usually between 5 and 6.6 kilograms (roughly 11 to 14.5 pounds), and the female, marginally smaller, weighing between 4.5 and 6.4 kilograms (10 to 14 pounds).

H. moloch is often thought of as one of the most endangered gibbon species, with estimates of its number ranging from a pessimistic 400 to an optimistic 4,000. Figures of between 2,000 and 2,500 are usually given. What makes that number especially ominous for their survival is that these numbers are distributed into geographically separated populations, none of which has more than 250 adults. The higher the number in each population, the greater the chances of survival.

This is why the few zoos that have *H. moloch* are seriously engaged in breeding programs. In 2010, Howletts and Port Lympne Wild Animal parks in Kent, England held 50% of the world's captive population of Javan gibbons, with 12 males and 13 females between the two sister parks. They have a quite active and successful program of breeding. In the summer of 2010, they had three juveniles: the young male Hirup, born on October 20, 2009, the even younger male Dwi (which means second son in the language Indonesian) born on March 21, 2010. Perhaps someday they will compete for the silvery affection of Baru (b. June 19, 2009), born of different parents.

In chapter five, you will read about an *H. moloch* family line that is singlehandedly contributing significantly to the successful survival of its species.

HYLOBATES KLOSSI

Siberut is an Indonesian island, one of the four Mentawai Islands off the west coast of Sumatra, all of them homes for *Hylobates klossi*. In *The Gibbons of Siberut*, Tony Whitten recounted the traditional myth linking the origins of *H. klossi* and humans. ("Beelow" is the name in the local language for *H. klossi*.)

> Long, long ago, when Siberut was the only island in the ocean, there was nothing but forest from . . . the north to . . . the south. . . . [A]nimals abounded and their life was easy. Life was so easy . . . that some animals found they were becoming too crowded. Even the tallest . . . trees were crowded and the beelow gibbons found there was not enough food for all. So they decided to call a meeting of all the beelow on Siberut to discuss the problem. Eventually, after many days of debate they all agreed that half of them should climb down to the ground and try to live there, and the other half should stay in the trees. In time, the beelow on the ground changed into men and thus became our ancestors.

When *H. klossi* was first "discovered" by Western science, they were identified as "dwarf siamangs." They even received the same genus name as the big guys. One major reason for this naming was that—like the vast majority of siamangs but unlike other gibbons—*H. klossi* are all black with no light-coloured markings anywhere. They were labelled "dwarf" as they are smaller than siamangs, just like all other species of gibbons. Unfortunately, some websites still refer to them as being small, even though their average size is well within the range of other gibbon species.

The common names for this species include Kloss's gibbon or Mentawai gibbon. The leader of the expedition that "discovered" them in the 1920s was English zoologist Cecil Boden Kloss. His work led to several plants and an owl being named after him, as well as the gibbon, one of the benefits of being a pioneering scientist. I would love to have a species named after me.

Kloss's gibbons are well-known in the scientific literature for their singing, even though, like *H. moloch*, they do not usually sing duets. One reason why it is a delight to read Whitten's work on *H. klossi* is his obvious love for the small primates, especially their singing. Two gibbons, Sam and Bess, are particularly featured in his descriptions. One morning at about four o'clock (you have to be a morning person to study gibbons in the field), he heard Sam begin to sing:

> It started with soft piping notes each separate from the last by as much as a minute. The pipes became longer, like long descending whistles, and then two or three whistles were joined together. Progressive elaborations of this theme so followed until fast ascending whistles became a short trill. Each phrase was not

necessarily the same as, or more complicated than, the preceding phrases because Sam often regressed to earlier phrases and began anew. Even when he reached the trill phrases, he rarely gave more than two in a row.

Whitten was treated to these wonderful performances once every other day. What further amazed him was that Sam's mate and their daughter could sleep through dad's solo song.

His description of Bess's solo was equally creative and appreciative. What made him all the more amazed by the performance was that while she entertained him with her song, she was climbing and swinging wildly through the trees (song and dance, singing and swinging):

> Then Bess made noises like a girl learning to yodel (unsuccess-fully). She floundered around for nearly a minute and then broke into her first introductory notes. Each lasted rather more than a second and was even pitched. She produced about forty of these notes each minute for several minutes. . . . Then, like a car being eased into third gear from a whining second, she flowed smoothly from the introductory notes into her full song. . . .
>
> The pitch of the notes rose slowly over about ten seconds, get-ting shorter and developing from simple hoos into whoops. Then the pitch stopped rising but the notes continued to quicken. . . . At the climax she was singing five loud, high notes every second. . . . . After about ten seconds of the trill she slowed down and the notes got longer, lower and quieter.
>
> Bess then sat down to rest but less than half a minute later she started again, this time without any introductory notes. This "great-call" lasted even longer than the first. . . . . Between great-calls Bess gave single whoops and sailed up to the notes of the great-call from these. Thus she continued for twenty minutes or so; the length of each great-call remained more or less the same but the gaps between them became longer and longer, presum-ably as she tired and became less inclined to rush around.

Bess would treat him to such a performance once every four days. And he agreed with someone he anonymously referred to as an *eminent gib-bonologist* that the song of the female *H. klossii* was "the finest music uttered by any land mammal."

Whitten believed, and I agree, that one role of the long singing is a demonstration of fitness. Anyone who can sing that long must be strong.

With male orangutans, their competitions in sound-making are known as "wahoo contests."

Whitten heard another story from the people concerning the inter-connection between humans and Kloss' gibbons. In my rewording it runs as follows:

There was once a couple with no children. Every morning the wife would go out to feed her chickens. Near the place where she fed them there was a tall tree that bore "the most wonderful red juicy fruit." As she could not, apparently, climb the tree herself to reach the fruit, she called to a gibbon she saw high in the tree, asking him to throw down some fruit for her to eat. He did as he was asked.

This happened every day until they fell in love (although falling is not something that the gibbon would like to do from a tall tree). And she became pregnant. Her husband, suspicious about the pregnancy, and also suspicious of the time his wife took in feeding the chickens, hid out of sight as she called the gibbon, asking for the fruit that he then tossed down.

After she left, the husband chopped down the tree, caught the gibbon, and cut off his head, placing it into the chicken feed basket. When he returned to their home he told his wife to be sure to look carefully into the basket the next time she went feeding the chickens.

When she returned to feed the chickens, after noticing that the tree had been felled, and not getting response to her call to her beloved gibbon, she looked into her basket, and was horrified by what she saw.

When she gave birth, it was to a male baby covered in long black hair (like the Kloss's gibbon father). He was called Sibulubulu, meaning "the hairy one." I'm glad my students don't know about that name.

The story goes on to tell of how Sibulubulu would be lazy and listless with his fur on, and handsome and hard-working when he took his fur off (an arrangement which eventually became permanent). The story emphasizes the similarity between gibbons and humans, as is also the case in other such stories.

Hoolocks

Two whoops. I stop dead in my tracks and listen. Silence. Another whoop. Another silence. And suddenly, in a burst of pure tones, the ancient symphony begins. The forest stills, overwhelmed, transfixed. Each time, these moments of the old song are new to me. These moments of the life-song of the hoolocks gibbon, echoing richly through the forest, scudding through the sunbeams, filling the heavens and stirring the earth. It is the call of the deep, dark rainforest.

The word *hoolock* is based on words from the South Asian languages of Hindi and Bengali—*uluk* in Hindi, and *ulluk* in the related language of Bengali. Local Indian names for the hoolocks also include terms translated as "little man of the forest" and "black man of the deep jungle." The Hoolock gibbons were named scientifically by American anatomist Richard Harlan (1786–1843) in 1831 as *Simia hoolocks*. Then, in the 1880s, they were re-branded *Hylobates hoolocks*. This was changed to *Bunopithecus hoolocks* in 2002, when a connection was made between hoolocks and the extinct gibbon-like fossil specimen *Bunopithecus sericus* found in southwest China. Recently it was discovered that Hoolocks are not as closely related to this fossil specimen as previously believed. So in 2006 their last name became their first name too: *Hoolock hoolocks*, at least for the western species. With all these name changes, it's good that they don't have ID cards to update. Informally, they are sometimes referred to as white-browed gibbons. As mentioned earlier, that is not a distinctive trait of any one species of gibbon.

There are two recently recognized species of hoolock: *Hoolock hoolock*, or the Western hoolock gibbon, and *Hoolock leuconedys*, or, wait for it, the Eastern hoolock gibbon. The former lives in the seven northeastern states of India, as well as in Bangladesh and Myanmar (Burma). It was thought until a 2006 sighting in the northeastern state of Arunchal Pradesh that *Hoolock leuconedys* was not found in India, but it is now accepted as living there, as well as in Myanmar and China.

Hoolock numbers have drastically fallen over the last few decades. A 2008 survey of the species estimated that there were only 282 left in Bangladesh. As of 2009, the seven zoos in India that have Hoolock gibbons only have 40 individuals. Over the last 40 years the population of western hoolocks in India has fallen by about 90%, down to a number of about 5,000, with perhaps a total hoolock population of 6,200 to 7,700 in the entire country. In Myanmar (or Burma), there are reckoned to be at least 5,900 gibbons, but in China there are fewer than 100. This would make for a total hoolock population of 13,700, extended over a very broad range.

Hoolocks are the second largest gibbons, being 60 to 90 centimetres in length and weighing 6 to 9 kilograms (13.2 to 19.8 pounds). Unlike most other gibbons, it is *relatively* easy to distinguish between adult males and females based on fur colour. To use the technical term introduced earlier, they are sexually dichromatic. The babies are born light-coloured (often described as "milky white") but their fur then darkens after about six months to a year. The females are black before puberty, but lighten afterwards, while the males are black throughout their adult lives. This is not an unusual sexual colour distinction—male black and female buff—as we will see in the discussion of Nomascus gibbons.

As is typical of all gibbon species, there is little difference in the sizes of males and females. Female western hoolocks' average body length is 48.3 centimetres or about 19 inches, while males are 54.2 centimetres or a little over 21 inches. Adult females weigh 6.1 kilograms or about 13.4 pounds, while the adult males tip the scale at a whopping (or is that a whooping?) 6.9 kilograms or a little over 15 pounds.

"HOOLOCK GIBBON: A GREAT SOCIAL WORKER IN THE FOREST"

One of my favourite books about gibbons is Chetry, Chetry and Bhattacharjee's *Hoolock: The Ape of India*, published by the Gibbon Conservation Centre in Assam, India. One reason for my appreciation of this fine book is a section entitled "Hoolock Gibbon: A Great Social Worker in the Forest." When I first saw the title for this section, I had no idea what it could possibly be about. The authors point out that as frugivores (remember that that means "fruit eaters"), hoolocks disperse seeds throughout the forest. It is kind of a trickle-down (or poop-down) effect. Secondly—and humans will appreciate this—they help control the number of insects in the forest. There is an insect-eating bird called a drongo, that looks a bit like a crow (it is typically black or gray), but is not a close relative. Drongos follow gibbons, for when the gibbons move through the trees the small apes disturb the insects that are resting on branches and leaves. When the bugs fly up, the drongos are ready to pounce. Everybody gains but the insects.

Thirdly, as we have seen, the hoolocks gibbons provide an important social function in giving off loud vocalization when large predators are near. They are like crows and jays in North America in that way. The gibbon alarm system warns everyone that there is danger nearby. You can't be a better neighbour than that (except to the predators).

THE HOOLOCK IN HISTORY AND LITERATURE

The naturalist and political administrator Sir Robert A. Sterndale (1832–1902), in his book *Natural History of the Mammalia of India and Ceylon*, published in 1884, wrote what he thought of hoolocks as pets, and how close his family came to one such pet hoolock:

> I think of all the monkey family [sigh!] this Gibbon makes one of the most interesting pets. It is mild and most docile, and capable of great attachment. Even the adult male has been caught, and within the short space of a month so completely tamed that he would follow and come to a call. One I had for a time, some years ago, was a most engaging little creature. Nothing contented him so much as being allowed to sit by my side with his arm linked through mine, and he would resist any attempt I made to go away. He was extremely clean in his habits, which cannot be said of all the monkey tribe. Soon after he came to me I gave him a piece of blanket to sleep on in his box, but the next morning I found he had rolled it up and made a sort of pillow for his head, so a second piece was given to him.

Although Sterndale had an influence on Rudyard Kipling in his writing of the popular *Jungle Book*, there are no gibbons in that book. In both Kipling's writings and in the Disney movie based on them, the King of the Apes character, called Louie by the Disney folks, was an orangutan, a species that is not native to India. The Indian gibbons are upstaged by those pushy orange-furred big apes.

However, John Lockwood Kipling, Rudyard Kipling's father, did make mention of hoolocks in his work *Beast and Man in India: A Popular Sketch of Indian Animals in Their Relation to the People* (originally published in 1891). He wrote somewhat negatively:

> The black gibbon (*Hylobates hoolock*), is better known in Bengal and Assam, and is well adapted for captivity. If a pair can be secured and the keeper does not object to a gentle, mournful and timid animal, the spirit of the complaining dove in the form of a black djinn or demon with a voice like a pack of hounds in full cry. The hoolock is monogamous, and seems to have few of the vulgar monkey vices, but is a depressing companion.

I disagree. They are anything but depressing. When I see and hear gibbons, it never fails to pick up my spirits. And I know that I am not alone in this.

Siamangs

> I first developed an interest in gibbons during childhood visits to the St. Louis Zoo. At the time a pair of siamangs . . . occupied the central display in the zoo's primate house. The cage was a stark enclosure, but a series of bars, shelves, and ropes allowed the occupants to showcase their speed and gymnastic abilities. When they were swinging around the cage, the siamangs captured the attention of almost all the visitors in the building, but during the remainder of the time, they were passed over for more visually conspicuous species such as prehensile-tailed spider monkeys, mohawked tamarins, or estrous baboons. But I was drawn to the siamangs over even the great apes, which were housed in a separate building. In the siamang's upright posture, round face, and pensive expression, I saw clear evidence of evolutionary continuity.

Siamangs were first described and named scientifically in 1778 as *Simia gibbon* by C. Miller. In 1821, siamangs drew attention—and a different name, *Simia syndactylus*—from Thomas Stamford Raffles. He would become the governor of Sumatra and British founder of the city/country of Singapore. The famous Raffles Hotel (where the drink the Singapore Sling was invented) was named after him. What would probably have been more important to him is the fact that his name is attached to the Raffles Museum of Biodiversity Research at the National University of Singapore, a place where, among other species, gibbons are studied.

Raffles appears to have had a siamang as a pet, as can be seen in the following passage:

> Besides the specimens in the collection, I have recently procured a living Siamang, which is very tame and tractable: in fact, he is never happy but when allowed to be in company with some one.

The name *siamang* seems to have come (or at least Raffles so believed) from the name given to one of the indigenous peoples of the island of Sumatra, with an alternative spelling of *samang*.

The formal scientific distinction at the genus level was made in 1841 by the German zoologist Constantin Wilhelm Lamber Gloger. He called siamangs *Symphalangus syndactylus*, both names being Latin/Greek constructions meaning roughly "fused fingers." One way in which siamangs differ from other gibbons is in having webbing connect the second and third fingers or toes on their hind feet. The feature is a bit like wearing small baseball gloves on your feet. I missed the fused toes in my first experience with siamangs, but saw them after careful observation later on. Even in a compound siamangs can move fast, their feet not easy to see.

Siamangs have other several points of difference from other gibbons. The initially most visible difference is size. It's almost as if they are gorillas and other gibbons are chimpanzee-sized, as siamangs are roughly twice the weight of their gibbon cousins, reaching weights up to 14 kilograms or 30.8 pounds. Their proportions are different too, with broader chests, higher faces, longer arms (relative to the length of their legs) and shorter legs (relative to the trunk of their body). Imagine if your arms were longer than your head-to-toes standing height. (At least it would be easy to tie up your shoes! You would not have to bend over.) Siamangs are only about one metre in height, but can look much bigger because of their thick black fur and the length of their arms. Their arm span—from the fingertips of their left arms to the fingertips of their right arms—extends between 1.5 metres and 1.8 metres, or roughly from not quite five feet to almost five feet, 11 inches. That last length is roughly my height before I started to get really old and shrink.

The second point of difference—and this is apparent both to the eyes and the ears—is that they have a vocal sac in the throat, called a *gular sac*, which gives both males and females a greater capacity to articulate loudly over long distances. You can think of it as an organic boom-box or amplifier.

Siamangs differ from other gibbon species in various smaller ways. Siamangs do not have the colour variety of their gibbon cousins. They are always black in colour, with reddish-brown eyebrows. Another difference is in their diet. They are the most *folivorous* of the gibbons. There's another "vore" for your vocabulary. It means that siamangs eat more flowers and other non-fruit vegetal matter than other gibbon species do. They still are very fond of fruit, however. The range that they travel through in a day is also substantially smaller than that of the other gibbons. That does not make them couch potatoes, however (or would that be canopy potatoes?).

They still will brachiate about one kilometre a day, more than many humans of my age and acquaintance walk during the same period of time.

And while we are talking about siamang behaviour, we have an account of a "typical siamang day," based on the fieldwork of David Chivers from 1969 to 1973, as published in his classic work *A Field Study of Primates in Tropical Rain Forest* (1974). The family written about here consisted of two parents and three children:

A TYPICAL SIAMANG DAY

6:00 a.m.—The adult male and juvenile awaken in the terminal branches of one of the tallest trees, followed by the adolescent in a neighbouring tree. Soon after they get up, they are joined by the adult female and infant.

6:10 a.m.—"After several minutes one siamang starts urinating, soon the air is full of falling excreta, as the group urinates and defaecates in concert [i.e., at the same time, not while playing instruments]."

6:20 a.m.—The adult male leads the family to a feeding tree and they all eat fruit. (He doesn't bring home the bacon, he guides them to the fruit.)

9:00 a.m.—The adults sing for about 15 minutes. They may sing again sometime later in the morning.

9:15 a.m.—Group grooming takes place for about half an hour. The groomer parts the long thick fur of the one being groomed, looking for lice or dirt to clean off of the fur.

9:45 a.m.—The adult female leads the group from feeding tree to feeding tree. The adult male carries the infant.

1:00-3:00 p.m.—In the full heat of the day, the group may take a siesta, or rest and groom.

5:00 p.m.—This is the final eating time of the day

6:00 p.m.—Usually by this time the members of the siamang family have found tall trees above the canopy of the jungle to sleep in. It is a good thing that they do not sleep walk (or sleep swing).

Good night, all. Hold onto that tree.

Siamangs live in the forests of Malaysia, Thailand, and the island of Sumatra in Indonesia. It is hard to know precisely how many siamangs remain today. They are bigger than other gibbons, and therefore a little easier to see, but they still stay high up in the trees. In 2002, it was estimated that in Bukit Barisan Selatan National Park in Sumatra, a protected area of 3,568 square kilometres, with about 2,570 square kilometres of forest cover, there were about 22,390 siamangs.

Nomascus

As we noted earlier in the chapter, *Nomascus* is the gibbon genus that has the greatest number of chromosomes, 26 pairs or 52 chromosomes in total. Again reviewing (I can't stop being a teacher), that chromosome number beats the other apes by four and whips us by six. There appear to be seven species of Nomascus gibbon, although there is no general consensus on this. Disagreement is a regular part of science. Sometimes members of the *Nomascus* genus are known as the *crested gibbons*. Three species have the word "crested" in their name. Nomascus species include:

- *N. anamensis* (northern buffed-cheeked gibbon)
- *N. concolor* (concolor or black-crested)
- *N. nasutus* (eastern black crested)
- *N. hainanus* (Hainan black-crested)
- *N. leucogenys* (northern white-cheeked)
- *N. siki* (southern white-cheeked)
- *N. gabriellae* (yellow-cheeked)

The name *Nomascus* first appeared in 1933, in the writings of early gibbon specialist Adolph Schultz (he was mentioned earlier in this chapter). I have read no source that indicates what the word means. That frustrates me. It is tied with *Hylobates* as the most "speciose" (I love that term) genus of gibbon.

NOMASCUS CONCOLOR (BLACK CRESTED)

This was the first Nomascus species to be identified, named *Simia concolor* by the American anatomist Richard Harlan, who also named the Hoolocks, in 1826. Everyone agrees as to its separate existence. In this genus that is something. It lives in isolated parts of China, Laos and northern Vietnam. The adult males are almost completely black, with some sporting white or buff cheeks (a gibbon fashion statement). The females are quite different looking, being primarily golden or buff coloured, with patches of black, particularly on the top of their heads (the black crest of their common name). You could not call them jungle creatures as they typically live in high altitudes (even without adding the height of the trees they sleep near the top of), too cold for jungle. They are critically endangered, with an estimated 1300 to 2,000 population remaining.

NOMASCUS LEUCOGENYS (NORTHERN WHITE-CHEEKED)

The second Nomascus species to be named, it was given the label "leucogenys" in 1840 by Irish lawyer and naturalist William Ogilby (1808–1873). It is a Latin term, with *leuco* meaning "light" or "whitish," while "genys" means "cheeks and chin": in other words, *light cheeks*. Up until 1989, as with the other *Nomascus species*, it was considered merely a subspecies of *N. concolor*. By 2004, it was considered a species, at first together with *N. siki*, as their songs are similar, and the females look very much alike. But now a separation between northern and southern seems to be favoured by most experts.

NOMASCUS SIKI (SOUTHERN WHITE-CHEEKED)

Nomascus siki lives in central Vietnam and southern Laos. The classification of this variety of gibbon has had a rather complicated history. For some scientists it remains unresolved. Over the years they have been considered subspecies of three of the other Nomascus species: *N. concolor*, *N. leucogenys* and *N. gabriellae*. Some have believed that it is a hybrid of the last two named. The evidence for separate species is genetic. It comes down to what is called *mtDNA*. The "mt" stands for *mitochondria*, a part of every human cell, and a part that has its own distinct genes, or DNA. *Mitochondrial DNA* is only passed down from mother to child. Dad has no input. The mtDNA of the two species is different enough to convince some scientists that *N. siki* is a distinct species. Stay tuned for some late-breaking scientific news.

NOMASCUS GABRIELLAE (YELLOW-CHEEKED)

With *N. gabriellae*, we have a neat example of sexual dichromism, each sex having different colouring. It follows a pattern you will by now have read about a few times. When they are very young, both sexes are light coloured. The males darken and stay dark. The females become buff-coloured or blond. The cheeks of both, however, have the same yellowish-buffy-gold hue, hence the species name. They are found in southern Vietnam, northeastern Cambodia and southernmost Laos.

When I first saw this name I wondered, and maybe you did too, who was the Gabriella they were named after?

In an informative and interesting article entitled "Gabriella's Gibbon," in the online *Gibbon Journal*, which often presents stories that are informative and interesting, Simon M. Cutting tells us the story of the name's origin.

The Western "discoverer" (remember how Columbus was supposed to have discovered America) of this species was Gabrielle Maud Vassal (1880–1959). She was English and well-educated. Her husband was 13 years older than she was, a dashing military-doctor-turned-scientific-researcher named Joseph Marguerite Jean Vassal. Four months into their marriage, as a member of the French colonial service, he was posted to Vietnam, a French colony. Gabrielle stayed with him there one year, but decided to return home to Britain for two years (they did remain married, however). She negotiated with the British Museum to sell for decent sums of money specimens of birds and animals that her husband collected, including the green magpie, now scientifically called *Cissa gabrielle*.

She returned to Vietnam in 1907. An adventurous spirit, she went on trips to indulge her scientific curiosity, without her husband, but accompanied by a guide and native servants. On one such trip, she encountered the gibbon that would bear her name:

> Sometimes the silence was broken by the shrill cries or loud wails of monkeys [gibbons!!!!!], and the branches above our heads shook and rattled as a family party took flight. We could not see them distinctly through the leaves, but my boy [manservant Da] shot two and brought them to me in triumph. They were both Gibbons, which are the only representatives of the man-like apes in Annam [Vietnam]. One was entirely black [i.e., a male] except for a buffy gular [from the Latin *gula* for throat, like the word "gullet"] patch, with long fur. It has since been named *Hylobates gabriellae* after me. It was a new species.

In 1909, the British Museum's Michael Oldfield Thomas declared "I propose to name it in honour of Mrs. Vassal, to whose help much of her husband's success in obtaining interesting animals has been due."

I find a lot to respect in Gabrielle Vassal; her courage, intelligence and independence of spirit come to mind. However, I am still troubled by her having the gibbon shot. I know it was common practice then, but it still bothers me. And calling a manservant "boy" also bothers me.

NOMASCUS NASUTUS

Nomascus nasutus, otherwise known as the Cao Vit or eastern black-crested gibbon, lives in the border area of Vietnam and southern China, two countries in which it once ranged more broadly. The scientist who first identified the species has one of the best (or at least the longest) names in biology: Philippe Alexandre Jules Künckel d'Herculais (1843–1918). Clearly he was not someone who would do well with a "Hello, I'm . . . " sticker on his shirt. Künckel d'Herculais (for short) was a leading French entomologist (insect specialist), who took time off studying bugs to identify this primate species in 1884.

In one of the very few times that gibbons have appeared in any sort of *National Geographic* publication, hard copy or virtual, it was on February 13, 2009 to announce that a baby *N. nasutus* had been born. This is quite an event, as it is estimated that there are only 100 to 110 left in the world, giving them a critically endangered status. For almost 40 years, they were even thought to have gone extinct. Then a remnant group was discovered in 2002 in Cao Bang Province, Vietnam.

An organization called Fauna and Flora International is active in trying to rescue this species from extinction. One of their measures has been the creation of the Cao Vit Gibbon Children's Festival. If there are any teachers reading this book, I think it would be a good idea to have a Cao Vit Gibbon Day at your school. It might help bring some desperately needed awareness of the plight of this disappearing species. Don't let them be invisible to your students.

NOMASCUS HAINANUS

N. nasutus is not the most endangered primate, however. That questionable honour goes to its sister species (or in some people's thinking subspecies), the Hainan black-crested gibbon (*Nomascus hainanus*). It appears there may be fewer than 20 individuals remaining, living on the island of Hainan, China from which the species' name is derived. This is a huge drop from the roughly 2,000 that are said to have existed in the 1950s.

Differences between *Nomascus nasutus* and *Nomascus hainanus*

	Adult male	Adult female
N. nasutus	Black with some brown on chest	Buff to beige with a black cap
N. hainanu	Entirely black	Buff to beige with a black cap and a white face ring that thickens above the mouth and below the eyes

NOMASCUS ANAMENSIS (**NORTHERN BUFFED-CHEEKED GIBBON**)

Members of this "new" species, identified in 2010, were earlier thought to be *N. gabriellae* (yellow-cheeked), as in appearance they seem to be virtually identical. Their DNA and their distinctive calls were used to distinguish this rare dweller of the borderlands of Vietnam, Cambodia and Laos from its near cousin.

Ending the Chapter

Before DNA analysis could be used and song variation became thoroughly studied, only visual evidence (often from a distance) served to distinguish different species of gibbons. Now it would seem that with better methods, we have more species.

We began this chapter with a quiz. Here are the answers to the questions:

1. The right answer is **d.**—there are four genera of gibbons.
2. We have a tie. It is both **c.** and **d.**
3. We have a (white)-hands down winner with **a.**
4. With arms the length of the height of an average human being (or taller), the siamangs win, fused feet down.

Now that the scientific presentation has been completed, you can read stories about some amazing gibbons that I have met. You won't be disappointed.

CHAPTER FOUR
Gibbons I Have Met

As a professor of anthropology, I have taught about gibbons for over 30 years. But until recently, I didn't teach much about them. Prior to embarking on this project, I was aware of no more than what little information about gibbons is presented in anthropology textbooks. I knew that they were apes, but were the ones that are most distant from humans. Of course, I knew that they had no tails. I had read that they were great at brachiation, swinging through the jungle trees, but I had no idea how they walked when they were on branches or on the ground. When I taught about these small apes, there was little more to be said, because there was little more that I had read about them. I needed to learn more. And I felt that books and articles did not provide enough insight for me into the nature of the little apes. I needed more than words. I needed to see them in the furry, long-armed flesh.

This project began in 2009 as a way of gathering some interesting information for the physical anthropology textbook I was writing, and some new and more thorough material for me to use in the classroom. I anticipated that my wife Angie and I would go to one zoo, the Toronto Zoo, to gather a little research material. I would then write a little bit about gibbons for the chapter on primates, and have a story or two to tell my students in class. That would be it. I little knew how easily both of us would be charmed by the small apes. But then, we little knew when we obtained our first parrot that we would end up with eight of them a few years later. We are suckers for little furry or feathered faces.

Meeting with the first two gibbons convinced me that I wanted to meet more of them, and that I should expand the project. I decided that I would go to every zoo within easy driving distance of our home in Bolton (a little north of Toronto) to visit gibbons in the habitat in which most humans see gibbons: zoos. This chapter brings together my impressions based on our short series of visits over a five-year period to six zoos in southern Ontario.

My writer's strategy involved observing the gibbons in their zoo compounds, and making notes on what I observed. I hoped that there would be at least one story in every zoo. Writer's strategies don't always work. A favourite writer of mine, William Least Heat Moon (a Native American belonging to the Osage nation), was putting together material for a book about driving across the United States. He thought it would be a good idea to park his camper on the main street of a small town and develop a story based on what happened over 24 hours. Nothing that he felt was story-worthy happened. His only story was that there was no story. Having read that, I worried each time I visited a zoo that I would find nothing that I could write about. But there was always some story that needed telling. There was love and rejection, family life and being thrown out of the family. There was certainly a lot of acrobatics. There was two-legged walking that was better than I thought it would be. There was humour, and there was singing, amazing singing. It was like I had opened up a book and all the stories within it took life in front of me. Gibbons may have no tails, but tales are easily attached to them. There need to be more of these tales written in the English language.

First Gibbons: A Visit with Lenny and Holly

The gibbons that Angie and I first met were Lenny and Holly, two white-handed gibbons (*Hylobates lar*) living in the Metro Toronto Zoo. We visited them in the fall of 2009. Both of us, no doubt, had seen the two of them in previous visits to the zoo, as they had been there for years. We just could not remember anything specific about them. They were invisible in our memories. Both of us could remember experiences with many other animals (meerkats, otters, orangutans and gorillas, to name just a few), just not the gibbons. I am sure that our experience was not unusual in that regard.

Following the signs, we saw "African Pavilion," with "Gorilla" written in big letters, and "Indo-Malayan Pavilion" with "Orangutan" featured equally prominently. But there were no signs with arrows indicating that we would soon see gibbons when we walked down this or that path. Fortunately, we knew that they would be found, with the more heavily advertised orangutans, in the Indo-Malayan Pavilion (which includes creatures from **Indo**nesia and **Malays**ia). As you may remember from earlier chapters, most gibbons call southeast Asia home.

That is where we met Bev Carter, the keeper in charge of the gibbons at that time. She told us that Lenny and Holly, the gibbons there, had been at the zoo for 26 years, both of them bred in captivity. Holly came from the Bowmanville Zoo, not far down the big highway to the east (and the location of a later visit), and Lenny came from an American zoo. Perhaps that is why he seems to like to sunbathe, as he did several times as we watched

Holly

them. Maybe he was from California. She was 37. He was 35. They would probably live until at least their early 40s. Both of them looked and acted strong and healthy to me, agile despite their age.

Bev informed us that they had no children, and they "didn't like each other very much." We observed that they never came close to each other at any time during our short observation period. Apparently,

they did sing, at daybreak and at day's end, but not in duets. As both had been raised in captivity, the songs they sang were a mixture of different recorded gibbon songs they had heard, a lot like we do in our cars and showers. We did not hear a peep or a hoo from either one during our time there. We were told that the keepers did not play any gibbon songs to Lenny anymore, for when they did, he would get excited, patrol the gibbon compound like he was looking for danger, and get quite aggressive with Holly. Maybe it was *gangsta* gibbon music.

When we first saw Holly, she was sitting with her legs crossed, looking like a short, furry fashion model. She was a light brown brunette, darker by a bit than the ash-blond Lenny. If we hadn't been told this, it would have taken us some time to distinguish who was the female, and who the male. We could have figured that out for ourselves once Lenny decided to do a little sunbathing. Holly is occasionally given a stuffed toy, which she carries with her and sometimes grooms. They only take it away from her once she has abandoned it. She may not have been raised herself by a parent gibbon.

According to Bev, the two gibbons did not readily show any signs of the manual dexterity (hand skills) that indicate intelligence in other apes. They even had trouble with screw-top lids. But then, so do I. However, researchers have observed gibbons performing some acts of dexterity that

I find amazing. They have been observed throwing and catching objects in their hands and in their mouth when they are as young as two, not yet mature. Apparently, young chimps cannot do that. I don't think that I could at that age either.

Evolution teaches us that body parts can specialize to perform one very important task, and when they do, then sometimes the capacity to do less important actions is sacrificed. Our primate capacity to touch and understand with the pads near the tips of our fingers came to us at the cost of claws as weapons. Brachiation would appear to trump manual dexterity in gibbons. You don't have to manipulate a branch, just swing from it, when you are a gibbon. And gibbons can do this before they are one year old (for instance, consider the story of Milly later on in this chapter).

Lenny

Bev believed that gibbon intelligence is there, but it is more hidden. They observe things very carefully. Lenny and Holly obtain some of their food from a container that requires some thought and the use of two hands to fish food from, but they are very adept at doing so. People who work in good zoos know that constant mental stimulus is vital for the health and happiness of smart animals. We have learned that fact ourselves raising parrots and border collies. I guess that means that they shouldn't be allowed to watch junk television. "There will only be nature documentaries for you, young gibbon. No game shows or reality shows. We don't want you falling out of the trees or off the ropes in your compound."

THEY WALK ON TWO FEET!

I was not fully prepared for how well and easily Lenny and Holly walked on two feet. There was no apparent awkwardness. This observation would be confirmed with every gibbon I've ever watched. Perhaps, as an anthropologist, I should have known that. But I had never studied gibbons before. In my defense, that fact is not covered in the standard textbooks I had read. I kept asking myself, how could a creature so distinct from us in other ways walk so much like us? The apes closer to us—orangutans, gorillas, chimpanzees and bonobos—all *knuckle walk*. That is, they alternate in their walking between feet and the large-sized knuckles of their hands. Do not try this at home!

Since discovering gibbons' *bipedalism* (from *bi* meaning "two" and *pedal*, referring to feet), I have read some early descriptions of this in the literature. As a teacher, I hate to admit that I did not do my homework on this one. The earliest description I found is the following, provided by a Dr. Burroughs of the East India Company who spent time in India observing hoolock gibbons. This letter was published in William Jardine's 1866 description of hoolocks:

> They walk erect; and, when placed upon a floor or in an open field, balance themselves very prettily, by raising their hands over their head, and slightly bending their arms at the wrist and elbow, and then run tolerably fast, rocking from side to side.

My favourite early account of gibbon bipedalism appeared in 1906, in which Ernest Ingersoll remarked on their skillful "human-like" way of walking:

> . . . when they do occasionally come to the ground, they show themselves to be able to walk erect and more human-like than any other ape, setting the foot down flat upon the sole, holding the long arms gracefully above the head, and so taking a rapid and funny gait. . . . Forbes had a tame siamang that used to accompany him every evening about the village plaza, learning elegantly on his arm, to the admiration of all the people; and a French writer describes how one would walk down the length of a table without disturbing a dish.

I don't think that I could do that. I would knock something over.

Lenny and Holly's only problem with bipedalism seemed to be that they had too much arm for walking, curving their arms up high, parallel to their heads. When they walked it looked as though they were trying to balance on a branch or tightrope and were very confident that they could. I am pretty sure that if someone gave them a skateboard, they would be good at balancing on that.

However, as smooth are their walking might be, it is as brachiators these gibbons truly impressed this human observer. Lenny and Holly could change from ordinary walkers to creatures of brachiating beauty when they would swing, apparently effortlessly, from branch to branch to metal arch in their compound. It would be interesting to see how they would do on human playground equipment.

According to Bev, Lenny and Holly have occasionally "brachiated right out of the compound, and have to be shouted back." The branches of the trees in their compound have to be regularly trimmed back to discourage such adventuring, and Vaseline was spread on the Plexiglas around the compound so they could not grab hold of it and escape.

After we left our furry friends, the first gibbons in our lives, we went to the gift shop. There you could see many primate stickers featuring chimps, orangutans and gorillas, as well as an orangutan tote bag and many, *many* stuffed monkeys. After looking for a while, we finally found one stuffed gibbon, which we, of course, bought. His (her) name is now Lolly, a combination of the names of the Metro Zoo gibbons. We may give Lolly to our grandchildren in the future. We may not. They will, however, get many opportunities to meet gibbons in zoos.

REVISITING LENNY AND HOLLY

We revisited Lenny and Holly late in July 2014. I phoned the zoo first, asking the morbid question of whether or not they were still alive. They would have aged five years since we last saw them, and they were already relatively old. I spoke with Andrea Beatson, the new keeper, and she was happy to tell me that they were still with us. I heard from her that the two of them were preening each other now. I hadn't known that before, and found it a little hard to believe given their mutual animosity. Further, they had made a few more successful escapes. That was easy for me to believe. Apparently, though, they weren't too pleased with their situation once they were out of the compound, and were easy to return to their home. I guess the figs are always greener on the other side of the Plexiglas.

When we went on July 31 to revisit Lenny and Holly, we couldn't find them at first. Twice around the Indo-Malayan pavilion we went, helped by no signs, no "this way to the gibbons" indicators. Finally, almost by accident, we were there, and we saw Lenny in the distance. It was a high school reunion with the shy kid that became even more introverted as an adult. I "knew" (or hoped I knew) that it was Lenny, as it is still hard for me to actually see the difference between male and female. I am out of practice. Once I saw Holly too, I could tell for sure. She's a bit darker, bits of black in her fur, and the lighter parts seem not as blond as Lenny's fur.

I repeatedly called his name. He moved forward in stages, turning his back at first after establishing each bold new move to a spot in the compound closer to the visitors. Then he would turn around slowly, looking our way, but not with his whole body turned towards us (just in case he had to flee suddenly).

His last step was to sit on a log by the water, the moat that holds the large Chinese soft-shelled turtles in, and the gibbons back. There he presented his back, then executed a shy half-turn as he looked down, frequently looking up at his audience for a few brave moments.

I taught a few kids passing by how to "hoo" softly to him, and he responded by looking up at them. I gradually developed an impromptu gibbon lecture for the passers-by that always began with "He's not a monkey; he's an ape." I was thanked a few times, and also I got to plug this book a few times.

As we left, I saw a sign that said "Turtles in Crisis," with a story board connected to it. I love turtles and have for decades, but this made me feel angry. Why didn't they have a sign like that for the gibbons? Is it because they are invisible?

There were several ways in which I saw gibbons being rendered invisible on this trip to the zoo. There were "Adopt a —" signs, but not one with the word "gibbon" or a picture of one. In the gift shop there was a primate postcard that didn't include a gibbon in the long list of primates. There was a book for children, entitled *Endangered Animals*. It contained no text about or pictures of gibbons. There were stuffed green and purple gibbons, but nothing on the tag or little card said what they were. I wrote "These are gibbons" on a piece of paper and stuck it on the display. At least for a short time people would know. We received at the entrance to the zoo a flyer entitled *40 Days of 40 Animals*. You get no points for guessing that there was no day for the gibbons. Their day has yet to come.

Introducing Miss P. (Penelope)

My absolute favourite gibbon (there goes the objectivity in this book) is Penelope or Miss P., a young black-furred, white-handed gibbon. You will remember her from the beginning of this book. Penelope was born on December 7, 2007 in Edmonton. Her mother, Julia, is a California blond, born in the Gibbon Conservation Center (GCC) in Santa Clarita, California in 1981. Penelope was her seventh child. As you may remember from the species chapter, the GCC is an important site of gibbon preservation (see also the section on Alan Mootnick in chapter seven).

Penelope's father's name is Chan. He is a beautiful, black male. Penelope and her brother Samson both have their father's colouring, as does their brother Bandit. Chan was born in 1992 at the Assiniboine Park Zoo in Winnipeg, Manitoba. He was sent out on breeding loan to the Edmonton Valley Zoo, when he was still sexually immature at two years old. There was some concern at that time that he was too young to be sent out to breed, but when he reached sexually maturity, he and Julia clearly hit it off.

The first time Angie and I saw Penelope, she had her thumb stuck in her mouth. She looked like a human two-year old that had just been scolded. That was a deceptive look. I think that she would respond to scolding with defiance, if anyone could get over her charm long enough to deliver a reprimand. She could get away with a lot.

Penelope

Penelope is very lucky to be alive. When her birth was approaching, she had the umbilical cord joining her to her mother wrapped around her neck. Knowing Miss P. as I do, I would almost suspect that she had been playing with it when it got stuck. They had to perform a caesarean section on her mother, Julia, so that both of them would survive the birth process. She weighed 401 grams, which is a little over 14 ounces. That is a little bit more than the small can of dog food we use to feed our dachshund and border collie.

Julia could not care for her child because of the incision, and because she lacked milk. The great dependence of gibbon infants on their mothers meant that someone had to care full-time for Miss P., including making sure that she got fed. That someone was zookeeper Andi Sime. For seven months, from Penelope's second day of life, Sime was her mother. Attempts were made to reintroduce Penelope to Julia, but the two simply did not seem to connect.

Sime's work was very difficult at first. The initial bottle feeding took 45 minutes, and the little ape only drank a few drops of human milk (I have no idea who the donor was). And Penelope would have to be fed once every three hours through the night. Sime acted and felt like any new mother with her first child:

> I had total mama jitters. I was so nervous. If she slept too deeply, I would check her. If she cried, I would check her. I checked her all the time and worried a lot.

Penelope bonded not just with Sime, but with her family pets:

> Penelope started grabbing the ears of the animals and enjoying the sensation of their fur. It was about touching and feeling. Then she would lay her hands on their heads and finally go in for a whole body cuddle.

When this intensive caretaking period was over, Sime was questioned by Janice Ryan, author of *Amazing Animals: Inspiring Stories about the Bond Between Humans and Animals*, concerning what she felt she had received from her experience with Miss P. Her reply was:

> Confidence. The prospect of raising an ape is mind-boggling. There is no manual. It was a blessing to be intimately involved with her life. Yes, it was an unnatural bond, but it was an honor. It was very intimate, being her primary caretaker, being the one, being her mom. The fabric of her life and mine were totally intertwined.

Perhaps Miss P.'s thumb-sucking could be a sign of her lack of gibbon maternal contact, as well as of her separation from her first adoptive mother. Perhaps her strong attachment to her giraffe blanket, now made into a hammock, is another such sign.

In April, 2009, Penelope travelled to the Bowmanville Zoo, almost 80 kilometres east of Toronto. There she met her first mate. There was some concern as to whether she would get along with Sandy, then 51 years old, a light brownish-blond, whose fur colour provided the inspiration for his name.

Sandy was a long-term resident at the Bowmanville Zoo. He had arrived there in 1963 as their first truly exotic animal, and their first (non-human) primate. His long-term mate, Ebony, had lived to the significant age of 46. Sandy had spent more than 43 years with her. As Ebony became weaker, Sandy showed himself to be the gentleman gibbon and great mate that he truly was. He would break the food given to him in half, to share with her. And he would open for her the lift-up door that separated the outside part of the compound from the gibbons-and-keepers-only part inside.

After Ebony died, the people at the zoo tried to fix Sandy up with a new partner, a six-year-old female, black like Ebony, but a different species, a black-handed or agile gibbon. The new prospective mate's name was Fufanu. Her story will be told later. From what I have heard, their relationship was like an extended, very bad blind date. They did not like each other. But they weren't forced to stay in each other's company. Fufanu went to a zoo near Niagara Falls, this time a home for a rejected and rejecting partner, not an escape for inseparable newlyweds.

Enter young Penelope. The first day of her arrival, the two white-handed gibbons sang their first duet. They bonded quickly, despite their difference in age, and in size. When I met them a year later, she was 4.5 pounds; he was 11 pounds. He was patient with her youthful exuberance for life. He had helped raise children.

BEING CHARMED BY PENELOPE

In the early summer of 2010, Angie and I arranged to meet with Penelope. The head keeper at the Bowmanville Zoo, Stefanie McEwan, came out of the gibbon building with Penelope snake-wrapped around her, thumb in mouth (Penelope, not Stefanie). Miss P. was very approachable while safely clinging to the security of her keeper. I could approach the young gibbon slowly and pat her very thick, black, slightly crimped fur, with no apparent concern on her part. She made no moves to bite me. As the owner of eight parrots, whose beaks have at various times left small scars on both my hands and my forearms, I have learned to early detect the signs of potential biting. I still get bitten, however.

Stefanie gave me a banana, not because I looked hungry, but to give to Miss P. in small pieces. Some pieces Penelope would grab with her mouth and small teeth. Her adult teeth were three years away. Then she would play a little "chew-and-show." Other banana pieces she would pick up with her long fingers (just a little bit shorter than young human adult Stefanie's fingers), plucking the banana pieces between thumb and upper palm. I don't think that I, or any other human I know, would be good at doing that. Try it and see.

As enjoyable as feeding her was, my first great Miss P. moment came later. My wife Angie has a gift for quickly sketching images of animals. She had brought her small artist's pad for that purpose. She wanted to draw a picture of Penelope with her thumb in her mouth (Penelope, not Angie). One problem that she has, like many artists, involves drawing hands. Hands are quite difficult to draw. As Penelope became more accustomed to us (the technical term is *habituated*), she felt comfortable enough with us to withdraw her thumb from her mouth. Angie had yet to finish the thumb-in-mouth part of her Penelope sketch, so she asked me to put my thumb in my mouth. I can't remember the last time I did that—perhaps after eating fried chicken. Looking around to see whether there was any-one who might see me making this unmanly gesture, I put my right thumb into my mouth.

Then it happened. Penelope reached over and rested her hand on my shoulder. I wondered how I should interpret that move. My thought was that she interpreted my thumb-sucking as a physical sign of my nervous-ness; perhaps I was a little scared. She could relate. She wanted to reassure me that I was among friends, gibbon and human. In my book (this book) that is called empathy.

The traditional scientific literature might call my interpretation *anthropomorphism*, inaccurately projecting human emotions and thoughts onto an animal. But much recent research reveals that apes have very similar basic thought and emotional patterns to our own, including empathy. The term for that way of thinking is *critical anthropomorphism*. Not recognizing such similarities is an attitude called *anthropodenial*. Over the next hour or so Penelope would reach over to me several times, touching my shoulder. I know that those were signs of friendship. I wanted to stretch out my arms and give her a big hug. I told the staff at Humber College, where I work, that I would have, but I did not want to scare her away. It would be only too typical of a human male to read more into a female touch than was really there.

Our relationship slowly progressed. Angie gave Miss P. a small scarf tied up in a circle. When Penelope dropped it, she jumped to the ground off Stefanie's shoulder to fetch it. Angie and I both crouched to observe her more closely, and we got our first group hug, Penelope's right hand on Angie's shoulder, left hand around mine.

There was more to come. After several shoulder touches and group hugs, I took a chance. She put her left hand on my shoulder. I tentatively reached out with my left hand, and she reached out with her right hand. I got my hug. It was short in duration, but long in impression. I was honoured with a literally touching gift. Then Penelope stood on my shoulder, as my parrots do. Now you know why she is on the cover of this book.

THE RECOGNITION EMBRACE

Early primatologist C.L. Carpenter, in the first major work on gibbons, wrote about the "recognition embrace":

> The two approaching animals come into an embrace in which, if the animals are swinging, they clasp one another with one arm and both feet; if they are walking they use their arms. As they come into the embrace, each gives a little cry which resembles a faint squeal, scarcely audible at a distance of 50 feet, which increases in pitch as the animals reach the climax of the embrace. The embrace lasts for only a few seconds, then the individuals separate.

Going to see Miss P. again, on July 1, 2010, was like going to a high-school reunion. Will she remember me? You never forget your first relationship with a gibbon. As we walked into the zoo, we saw the little black primate spidered out on the arms and shoulders of Jackie, a young blonde "zoo crew" staff member. I tried to look as unthreatening as a bear-built, bearded anthropologist can look. So like an active, curious child, she looked our way, her eyes very active. Then she looked away. Suddenly it happened: recognition. She dropped down from the sanctuary of Jackie's arms, and toddled excitedly, rapidly to me, arms up, reaching out for a big hug, which lasted a few seconds. She *eeed* and welcomed Angie and me with one of her group hugs. We followed her, with Jackie, to an eight-foot stump, a favourite exercise spot for Penelope. Several times she would jump into my outstretched arms to be boosted up towards the stump. She certainly didn't need the help to climb it, but we both enjoyed the game. Memories flashed back of playing with young family members, "tick tock, nephew clock," with a laughing child being swung like a pendulum (his mother not being in the room). Penelope and I held hands. She then suspended herself, with both hands grasped around my right arm. I held my arm up high, making it as much like a branch as I possibly could.

Penelope is something of a video star. You can see her on our YouTube video, "The Steckleys Visit Penelope the Gibbon," and you can also view a video of her March 16, 2012 taping of the *Steven and Chris* show on CBC. I think she liked us better. See what you think.

SANDY

Sandy met us as if he were the star of the circus and we were the adoring audience. Sandy was raised in front of an audience and grew up in show business. He liked to put on a show. We admired his performance as he circuited the compound, brachiating from rope to rope, then to the fence wall and back to the rope. Sporadically glancing back at us, he appeared to be seeking our attention and praise. "Are you watching me? Then look at this." He seemed to only do circuits when he was being watched. The more we cheered him, wowing him on, the more vigorously he swung through the compound, hooing as he performed. Sandy may have been a senior, but he was still an energetic and fit acrobatic performer when we saw him. We are glad that he was able to have one last strong summer before he died.

Sandy, who passed away in 2011, at 52, was not the oldest zoo gibbon on record. This prize goes to Nippy, a male Müller's gibbon (*Hylobates muelleri*) who is reckoned to have been at least 60 years old when he died in 2008 in the Wellington Zoo in Wellington, New Zealand.

Penelope now has a new partner. His name is Tyler (son of Mumma and Homer). He is an *H. agilis* on exhibit loan from Safari Niagara. Before our return to the Bowmanville Zoo in 2014, I suspected that despite the challenges of being with the energetic Penelope, the two of them would get along better than Sandy did with Fufanu. At the very least, they are much closer in age. We will be speaking of Fufanu in the section on Safari Niagara.

RETURNING TO PENELOPE

It was the summer of 2014. I was looking forward to returning to Penelope, seeing our furry granddaughter again. There was also mild concern. Would she remember me? Would I even recognize her? She would have grown and matured from being a child to an adult in the four years that we were apart. I had merely gotten older during that time.

When we met zoo employee Sandra Brownelle, she told us of her first experience with Miss P., which very much paralleled our own. "The first day she came, I held her and I just fell in love with her. She is just so special." This sentiment would be echoed by Andrew Cordier, who had done a one-year co-op placement with the zoo, when he spoke of his first contact with her. She charms everyone.

I recognized her at first sight. It was so obvious to me that she was Penelope, but I can't tell you why. She was much bigger now, like someone you remember as a little girl now standing in front of you as a 17-year-old. She was even bigger than Tyler, who is one or two years younger than her. She came down from her high spot on the top right hand corner to the ground. She walked around the circular objects that are there to enrich her living environment, and hid behind one of them.

She moved slowly around centre stage of the compound. I saw no look of recognition, but I didn't really expect to see one, just hoped for it. Occasionally she would lie on her back. Sometimes she would put her thumb in her mouth, but just as far as her now-larger teeth, no further. I wondered whether it was just habit rather than the indication of nervousness it was when we first met her. The behaviour was imprinted, and could have changed meaning.

She was idly plucking grass, sometimes chewing a bit on the blades. Guests of the zoo would occasionally throw her some "monkey cookies." Once she went over to one of the biscuits, picked it up, and carried it over to some water-holding device and dropped it in. According to Andrew, she would often dunk these biscuits in water before eating them, while Tyler was more likely just to bite off a bit and then toss it. That's such a guy thing.

She didn't seem to be paying as much attention to Tyler as he was to her. Not only was she bigger than him, but she appeared to me to have all the power in the relationship. I had heard from several people that they had fought when first introduced to each other, but did so a lot less often now. Stefanie McEwan told me that they would even sometimes preen each other.

SECOND RETURN VISIT
She spent much—maybe most—of her time with her thumb in her mouth. Tempted by her favourite, peanut butter, she approached the cage twice for this treat, both times touching hands with Angie, showing that she recognized her, but she backed away when I approached. She looked at me, but the contact wasn't quite there yet. I am someone she might think she should remember but doesn't quite.

Apparently she and Joel, an 18-year-old human male are very, very close. She sits down and sticks her feet out so that he will tickle or massage them. And she likes a belly rub like our dachshund Trudy does, but she demands it more aggressively than Trudy does with me, pushing up against Joel.

Females seem to be perceived as competition for her now, not like when she was young and they were all mothers to her. She is now more aggressive with them than she ever was before. Amanda Catherwood, another zoo staff member, told me that Penelope rips at Stefanie's hair when Stefanie comes too close to Joel. Penelope has also pulled at Amanda's ponytail, which obviously makes an irresistible target. And Miss P. has actually taken selfies. She looks at herself in the image finder and then clicks the picture.

I noticed a couple of other things that have changed apart from her size. She is a better biped now than when she was younger. Her legs are amazingly straight when she walks, and when she stands, she can look very much like that fictional being, the Sasquatch, only downsized. Our little granddaughter has grown up.

We Meet Tyler

We finally got to meet Tyler in August 2014. He was very quiet and shy when we first encountered him, sitting in the righthand back corner near the gibbon building and its promise of safety. He looked over his shoulder

Tyler

in the now-for-me classic gibbon shy pose. Knowing that he was being watched, he took to action after about 10 or 15 minutes. He went to the top of the compound and hung in the now-familiar gibbon pose of observation and showing-off. He made a series of sounds I don't remember ever hearing before from a gibbon, a kind of small-animal or baby-animal whimper but happier, kind of like the sound made by one of the squeaky toys that Brenda, our cat, likes to play with.

Tyler began to survey his audience the way Sandy used to do. Angie went over to him to take his picture, but also to talk to him, using the quiet hoos that we had heard from other gibbons. Then Tyler's hoos began, perhaps a sign of more confidence in his situation. Then he started to sing, experimentally with only two tones at first, then growing in range and in experimentation. I wonder whether he expected Penelope to respond to or share his song. A woman who was a daily visitor at the zoo told me that he often sings, but that Penelope rarely does. She couldn't remember whether she had ever heard the two of them singing together.

Tyler was quiet for a while. I wonder whether too many of my "good boy, Tylers" caused him to clam up. He was in what appeared to be his favourite spot, high spot in the left-most side of the compound, opposite the gibbon building. His singing made me wonder whether he was named after Steven Tyler of Aerosmith fame. He varied his song, playing with it in small different ways.

While I am watching and listening to Tyler's song composition efforts, I encounter and talk to Andrew Cordier, the co-op student mentioned earlier, who tells me some stories about young Tyler. Whenever Andrew put fruit or water in a container in the gibbon building for Tyler and Penelope to eat, Tyler would come flying down from a high spot, and give Andrew a "gentle" swat. He was also very protective of Penelope. He would give Andrew a smack if he felt that Andrew was getting too close to his mate.

While Andrew and I were standing and talking, Tyler came down to the front part of the compound, grasping the cross-wires of the cage with his hands and feet, pushed off a bit, and then peed directly downwards. I wonder if this was some kind of "I remember you, but don't mess with me" type of greeting. I'm glad that human males only do this metaphorically.

SECOND VISIT WITH TYLER

In this visit Angie and I learned that Tyler is the master of the slap-and-run. He does that with Joel, who is Penelope's new special friend, now off to vet school. Tyler sometimes taps him on the shoulder, like that old human trick of tap-and-hide, or hits him in the leg when he least expects it. There is some jealousy there.

He is sneaky. Angie was up close against the cage trying to get a good picture of Penny. Tyler stealthily approached the cage, neither of us sees him, and slapped Angie on the top of the head, and she definitely did not see it coming. We laughed, as a 10- to 12-pound gibbon does not pack much of a slap. The greatest impact came from the surprise.

Tyler has his eyes on me the whole time, sometimes sneaking up, looking for a way to get me in the leg or the shoulder or the head. It never happened. That was in part because my informant Amanda Catherwood kept warning me when he was coming.

Apparently, although he is younger and smaller, Tyler seems to be dominating in the food category. The staff have to be sure that she gets her share and that he doesn't steal it away. Both he and Penelope seem to prefer peanut butter to anything else. I can relate.

Runaround Fufanu

Here is the story, furry but true, of Runaround Fufanu. (Apologies to Dion, who in the 1960s sang "Runaround Sue," with the opening line, "Here is my story, sad but true. . . ."). Fufanu (like Tyler) is a young *Hylobates agilis*, otherwise known as a black- or dark-handed or agile gibbon. Fufanu lives in Safari Niagara, a zoo that houses white-handed and dark-handed gibbons, as well as a great collection of siamangs.

Our expectations concerning Fufanu were uncertain. We wondered if there was something *wrong* with her. After all, hadn't she rejected Sandy? Or was it the other way around? How could she not like Sandy? One reason may have been that they were different species. Both belong to the genus Hylobates, but Sandy was an *H. lar* or white-handed gibbon, while Fufanu is an *H. agilis* or black-handed gibbon.

Our opinion of Fufanu changed quickly. Even before we were officially introduced to her by Lana Borg, the animal care manager, we discovered that the lovely Fufanu was charming in her quiet way. Kind of shy, she swung quietly in the corner of her compound, showing us that she was truly a gibbon. She made small vocal sounds rather than the boisterous "hooing" repertoire of louder gibbons. Soon, in full view, she brachiated around the compound and came front and centre to meet her audience and communicate. She was definitely in our faces. Now her vocal sounds were louder, kind of an "ah–ah–ah–ah." Our niece, Eva, described it as "like a whimper, but more upbeat." Eva has a Ph.D. in chemistry, so I trust her scientific opinion, even though in this case it had nothing to do with the periodic table.

Now foolishly feeling that I was "good with gibbons" after experiencing two couples in two different zoos, I gave myself credit for Fufanu's being comfortable around me. However, as Lana informed us, the young female gibbon was in her estrus period. In other words, she was in heat. She might be comfortable with any male that gave her some attention. It was her, not me.

The Kingfisher: To Hoo or Not to Hoo

The second gibbon meeting at Safari Niagara was with the impressive Kingfisher, Fufanu's mate. Kingfisher is all black except for his white eyebrows. Those of you under 50 might wonder why an almost all-black animal would be named after a blue bird. In fact, he was named after a formidable character, Kingfish Stevens, in *Amos 'n' Andy*, first a radio and then a television show that was very popular from the late 1920s to the end of the 1950s. The role was played by a very funny African-American TV star, Tim Moore. I still do imitations of his formidable voice, particularly his declaration "Hello dere, Sapphire."

The gibbon named Kingfisher showed us right from the beginning that he had a flare for the dramatic. He made a great theatrical pose at the gibbon entrance to the compound with arms up high in a V-shape and body hanging down. He then swung through the branches from place to place while grabbing the protective mesh of the compound, living up to the reputation of being an *agile* gibbon. He hooed softly as he travelled. Later, when he was done, he and I exchanged hoos.

I wish that I had read the following passage from Thad Bartlett's fieldwork with white-handed gibbons in Thailand before vocally interacting with Kingfisher:

> After detecting the presence of a neighbor in the vicinity of a territorial boundary, the adult male quietly approaches the border area. On reaching the territorial border the two opposing males sit or hang within view of one another uttering a quiet series of staccato hoots. As the encounter develops, the quiet hoots may grow into a louder and more-sustained full solo call. Generally one male will then displace the other by entering the other's tree. This continues back and forth until one of the males initiates a sudden but brief chase.

Among the "antagonistic gestures" of gibbons identified by pioneering primatologist C.R. Carpenter was what he called "characteristic rage behavior of shaking supports or stamping up and down repeatedly." A primatologist watching Kingfisher and me interact might have written the following field note:

> After detecting the presence of a large, bearded stranger in the vicinity of his cage, Kingfisher, the adult male, quietly approached him, softly hooing as he did. On reaching the side of

the compound beside the stranger, Kingfisher uttered a quiet series of staccato hoots. These were returned by the bearded stranger, ignorant of what he was saying, but confident in his ignorance. Kingfisher backed off until, prompted by the stranger's hoots, he aggressively swung toward him, hooing and then hopping up and down close to the compound mesh wall. The stranger then left. Kingfisher had successfully defended his territory. The foolish bearded stranger had been repelled.

The next time I went to Safari Niagara to observe the gibbons, as I walked up to the compound housing Kingfisher and Fufanu, I wondered what this new encounter would be like. Kingfisher was inside the building, so I didn't get to show him that I was no threat. In the next compound, a male infant and I hooed to each other, free of aggressive gibbon displays (stamping or shaking), on my or his part. We may both have been trying to sound non-threatening.

Coco, Sprog and Giggle: Happy Siamang Families

The teacher in me compels me to briefly review what was said earlier about siamangs. They are the King Kongs (or is that the Kings Kong?) of the gibbon world. Siamangs weigh in at about twice the size of other gibbons, topping the scales at over 10 kilograms (more than 22 pounds). They are unique among gibbons in other ways, too. First is their throat pouch that enables their singing voices to carry for miles and miles. They are more *folivorous*, meaning that they eat more grass, shoots and leaves, than other gibbons. They can pick up grass with their feet. (I wonder if they would help us with our weeding at home.) Their big toes are like thumbs. And dads play a significant role in parenting.

At first the infant is under mom's exclusive care. The two sleep together in the same tall tree, sometimes more than a hundred feet in the air. The infant hangs onto mom like it is a matter of life or death (it is!). Then, when the infant starts to roam around and get into mischief, say after about six months, dad takes over. Dad and infant are never far apart. That is what I had read, and I would soon see evidence backing up my reading.

When Angie and I went to Safari Niagara (where they have more siamangs than in any other zoo in North America) we first saw siamang dad Cocogog (Coco for short) sitting with five-month-old Gigglegog (Giggle for short) perched on his father's knees. For the half-hour to an hour that we observed them, they were never more than an arm's length apart.

Of course with gibbons, an arm's length is like a long leash. Mom (named Sprog) was relatively free to roam around by herself, although she usually stayed pretty close to the other two. They looked like a happy family.

Now I will tell you how a young adult siamang, Ognat, might disagree with that last statement. He might start his story this way: "There was once a happy family of mother, father and child, and then 'it' came into their lives. . . ."

Ognat's Sad Times and a Happy Ending

You just read about a happy family of siamangs at Safari Niagara. Now it is time to present a darker picture. (Actually *all* pictures of siamangs are dark as both males and females are almost completely black.)

You have just read about what a good father Coco was with young infant siamang Giggle. Coco had had practice with his first-born, Ognat. But Ognat was not with them when we went to visit. Where was he? And why was he not with the others? Here's the story.

Remember that gibbons live in a nuclear family. That means that generally there are only two adults in the gibbon group. Once gibbon children reach adolescence at age four and are well on the path to being adults, their parents begin to treat them differently. If they reach for food and both an infant or juvenile gibbon and their parents are nearby, the parents may threaten the adolescents or even hit them to keep them away from the food. The greatest conflict within a gibbon family unit detected by primatologists who study gibbons is between parents and adolescents. That seems a lot like humans. The younger ones get away with a lot. Not so the adolescents. Eventually, they are driven out of the territory. If they live in zoos, they are put in separate compounds.

There is good news, however. Ognat can attest to that. He experienced the conflict. He was taken to a separate compound, away from the others. But by 2010, when he was five, he was happily paired off with nine-year old Buri. He still showed some signs of his unhappy last times with his parents. When he is fed, he runs away to the back of the compound so that no one will take his food away from him (not that Buri would take food from him!). Don't worry, Ognat. There is no little one with parental backing who will steal your food. It's all yours, buddy.

On our second visit we witnessed a telling and moving scene. It was in late August, about five o'clock, approaching evening. Sprog, who had been brachiating across the compound, stopped and hung from the top at the building-end of her compound. We wondered what had drawn her atten-

81

tion. We looked at the other side of the building. There, at the top of the other compound, just yards away from Sprog, Ognat was looking back, his eyes directed towards his mother. It was a very beautiful moment, a mother-and-child reunion. I wondered whether such moments also took place in the wild.

Jojo's Happy Ending: A Gibbon Never Forgets a Friendly Face
This is the story of Jojogog (Jojo for short). In 2010, he was a 17-year-old adult male siamang. The young lad came to Safari Niagara from Howletts Wild Animal Park in southern England, a place that plays an important role in the breeding of endangered gibbons and sending them to zoos across the world.

Jojo's life in Canada began with sadness. He had travelled across the Atlantic with his father Gog. You now know about the close relationship between siamang infants and juveniles and their fathers, who take an active role in the raising of their furry offspring. Gog died of a blood clot in his heart shortly after their trip. That would have broken Jojo's heart.

Poor Jojo was alone in Safari Niagara until four more siamangs from Howletts arrived. Two of them were already a mated pair, but the other two were single adult females.

Lana, the animal care manager at Safari Niagara, did her homework (teacher's message here!), checking the history of the two newly arrived females. She discovered that one of them, named Kukugog, had been housed and mated with Jojo back in England.

Inspired by this information, Lana put the two gibbons together in the same compound. As we've seen, this can often be a tense moment for a gibbon couple. Since gibbons can display rejection of each other quickly and violently, the zoo staff were prepared for a possible battle. Would the siamangs from England recognize each other after years apart? Well, you never forget your first love. They are currently residing happily-ever-after in a compound-built-for-two at Safari Niagara (down the road from Niagara Falls, a traditional honeymoon backdrop for young lovers).

Samson and Carmen
On June 3, 2010, Angie and I went to Jungle Cat World, east of Toronto, in Orono, about 20 minutes away from Penelope in Bowmanville. There we met Penelope's older brother, Samson, who was almost eight years old, and a 15-year-old female, Carmen, both of whom were black-coloured *Hylobates lar*. "Sakura," the name on the sign, hadn't been changed yet.

We discovered that Sakura was Carmen's daughter, and had moved to the Calgary Zoo. There, the long-armed beauty is happily mated with Tunku, a blond from the University of Hawaii. I wonder whether a gibbon could combine surfing with brachiating.

Samson came to Jungle Cat World in the fall of 2008, along with an information sheet about him, the so-called "Enrichment Data Transfer Form." One key to his nature, and, I think, a form of proof that he is definitely Penelope's brother, is the following passage found in that form: "Samson is a very playful gibbon. He likes to sneak up and bang on the windows when the keeper is not looking. He will also look for specific keepers to play this game with. . . ." Further along, we also read:

Samson

> Samson really likes to play with keepers through the windows. We play hide and seek. Sometimes we sneak up on him and he will pretend to be scared. When we turn our back he will sneak up behind us and hit the window then swing away. He likes to play with his father [Chan] by wrestling and chasing him across the exhibit.

He is sneaky, as I learned on our second trip to visit him, and he made several quick swipes at my beard as I stood close to the cage.

Unfortunately, he was approaching that time of life when the relationship between father and child could become stressful. That is probably one good reason he was sent east to get a mate.

Samson also likes reaching into boxes that have treats hidden inside them. This seems to be a much-favoured zoo gibbon game. I can relate to that, as, when I was a child, there were often prizes in cereal boxes.

He is also quite an athlete. With his skill and joy in racing around his compound, he is the kind of competitor who would win gold for Canada if Run-Jump-and-Swing (Gibbons Only) were an Olympic event.

THE SAMSON AND CARMEN SOUND SHOW

Samson and Carmen were at first by far the quietest of the residents of the primate section of the zoo. The black spider monkeys sounded like Lime, our shrieking yellow-headed Amazon parrot. The lemurs, nearby, scurried about making their many small noises, sounding like an entire Madagascar jungle all by themselves.

The initial sound that we heard from Samson and Carmen was a soft hooing when their three o'clock meal arrived. That was nothing compared to what was to come. As you know, gibbons are great singers. The duets of mated pairs haunt the jungles of gibbon territory, and start the work day with songs for the early-morning zoo staff.

It is difficult to find words to describe the sad and beautiful sounds that we were about to hear. Just after the gibbons finished eating, they slowly worked up into a duet, a gibbon *Glee*. Carmen led the way with a call that sounded like a tube trombone. Samson's initial response to the lady gibbon's overture was a monotonal hoo. I noticed that they gestured differently when they sang. When he sang, his eyebrows went up. Hers did not. He pursed his lips when he sang. She did not.

What made the performance especially dramatic was that the gibbons did not sing alone. Shortly after the gibbons started their duet, another duet came in response. From across the far side of the zoo came the howling of two young timber wolves. They may have come from opposite ends of the world, southeast Asia and Canada, but these two very different species can still sing together.

Then Samson cranked it up a notch. His call became louder and lasted longer. Carmen responded in kind. The most dramatic part of their duet was like a fireworks rocket going off. It rose from lower to higher pitch, ending with a whistle. Unfortunately, as the duet intensified, I lost track of who was who (and who was hooing). It seemed to me that Samson was giving off the most dramatic calls. However, I had several times read that it is the females who have what is termed the "great call," generally the most spectacular part of the duet. Perhaps Samson was a cross-caller. Raised in zoos, maybe he learned to imitate the calls of females because those were the only calls he was familiar with.

Gibbon duets can last a long time. In the Gibbon Wildlife Sanctuary, duets have been recorded as ranging from nine to 33 minutes, averaging between 15 and 20 minutes. Of course, they don't need to memorize any words. Carmen and Samson's duet lasted only about two or three minutes, short for a gibbon song, but it still very much impressed Angie and me. I suspect that their early morning songs would go on much longer.

RETURNING TO SAMSON IN 2014

When first we saw Samson on our return in 2014, he was sitting up in the leftmost back corner. He was alone, as his mate Carmen had died. Since her death the good people at Jungle Cat World have been trying to find him a mate. He hasn't taken a liking to anyone yet. This is not unusual, as you will learn with Mary, the Müller's gibbon you'll meet in the next chapter. He was not shy with us for long. Soon he swung down to see us, a move also encouraged by the fact the zoo staff member was offering him grapes. I noticed that he was quite dexterous with his fingers, more than any gibbon I had seen before. Maybe I was too influenced by the developing but not yet developed child-gibbon Penelope that is his sister. Like his sister, he did the "shake your sillies out" move several times, with arms and head looking like they had been soaked and needed a shaky drying out.

Samson has this pose that makes him look both cool and intelligent. It was a pose that I had not seen another gibbon make. He sits on his swing with his hands upon his knees and his feet crossed one over the other (I don't think that I could do that last bit). He looks out at you with those deep brown eyes, and you could easily imagine him thinking something profound about the meaning of life, perhaps "To swing is to live. And to live is to swing."

He is a master on the swing. He jumps up and straddles the swing, so that he moves side-to-side when the swing moves back-and-forth. At first he does it with no hands on the ropes, but once the swing starts slowing down, he puts his right hand on the rope, ready for his next move. He was showing off for Angie, doing several "two times around the rope" circling swinging movements while her camera was on him. He is a performer.

A Story of Willy, Lily and Chilly

Writing down observations is a voyage of discovery, both about what you are observing and about yourself. You don't know what you're going to see until it appears right in front of you. You don't even know whether you will see something meaningful. You could end up like William Least Heat Moon (I mentioned him earlier) and see nothing that makes up a story. But I needn't have worried. The gibbons never failed to present me with stories.

Observing gibbons like the white-handed gibbons found in almost all the zoos that we visited brings with it the added difficulty of not knowing the sex of the gibbons you are studying. Both sexes have the same colour options, and both are about the same size. There are no huge silverbacks, as with gorillas, nor the facial flanges that make dominant adult male orangutans look like they have a large plate in their mouths. Fortunately, shortly after arriving at the Elmvale Zoo, we were told the names and gender of their three white-handed gibbons, Willy (the dad), Lily (the mom) and Chilly (their daughter). Willy was black with a bright white face. Lily and Chilly were both buff-coloured blonds: big and black = dad; big and blond = mom; smaller and blond = daughter. I got it.

In my admittedly limited experience with gibbons, I had never seen so much grooming. This involves a lot of parting of thick fur, rather like wading through tall grass looking for something (maybe like a golfer looking for a lost ball). When we first saw the gibbon trio, they were on a corner platform about 15 feet high. Two long planks formed a triangle with the two cage walls. Chilly was in the middle, being groomed by both parents. She was lying on her stomach with her back legs hanging down, enjoying the experience, but looking like she would take off at any moment. This child grooming lasted for a few minutes, followed by a short mutual group groom, and then Willy swung off. The two females remained on the planks, lounging on their backs high in the air as if they were at some exclusive gibbon beach. They too left after about five minutes. Throughout the time I observed them they never stayed still for longer than that.

About 20 minutes later, after all had travelled around their compound a bit, they were back, this time with Willy in the middle. Chilly left first this time; after all, she wasn't the one being groomed. Willy groomed Lily for about three or four minutes. Willy appears to be a well-practiced groomer, and would make good money if there were gibbon spas. He parts fur skillfully with his long fingers, searching and then grabbing offending objects (insects?) with his teeth. In comparison, young Chilly seemed more to go through the motions with her hands. She knows what grooming looks like, but she didn't seem too sure of why she was doing it, or what constituted good grooming. I had the same problem as a child with brushing my hair.

Members of this gibbon family were also skilled brachiators, especially father and daughter. Willy, who was 22 that summer, could swing faster than any gibbon I had seen to that point. He could fling himself from one rope to another some eight feet away with no trouble, and without having to build up any speed beforehand.

Chilly was impressive, too. She flung herself at least six feet in the air between ropes once. Sometimes she would build up momentum, rather like a human child pumping on a swing, by swinging her butt back and forth a few times before she took off.

IT TAKES A LOT OF WORK TO BE A GIBBON MOM

It takes a lot of work to be a gibbon mom. I first learned this when I watched Lily and Chilly play-wrestling on the high platform corner where they had earlier done their grooming. Chilly looked quite serious when she grabbed mom's foot with her teeth, but Lily exhibited less aggression when she seized hold of her daughter, almost gently, by the ear.

One scene in particular taught me about gibbon mom patience. You will remember that gibbons are frugivores, eating mainly fruit, but they also eat grass. Lily was the most dedicated grass-gatherer of the family. She worked hard to pull enough of the right kind of grass to fill her long-fingered hand. It is not easy to pull grass up in chunks. Anyone who has weeded using just their hands knows this. One time the grass was so hard to pull she had to lean back and grab a pole to anchor her. The time I remember the most clearly involved the following social scene. As Lily was preparing to eat her hard-earned blades of grass, Willy came along and pulled some grass out of her hand, as if she was a waitress offering her some (she wasn't). She didn't appear to complain when he did this. Then Chilly came along and tried to do the same thing. Mom resisted twice by quickly pulling her hand away from the reaching fingers of her demanding daughter. Then she gave up the fight. Did I hear her sigh in frustration? She let her daughter take some of her hard-won food. Change the grass to French fries, and you can see this scene take place with humans in fast-food outlets every day of the week. Gibbons are a lot like humans in so many ways.

One further note about gathering food is necessary here. Karl Kasper of the Elmvale Zoo told us that the gibbons had learned to make smart choices in their locally gathered foods. They (I suspect most probably Lily) had learned to pick and eat fresh dandelion leaves and ash leaves. This innovative discovery of what is decent food points to a good learning capacity in these apes far away from their traditional habitat. How many humans could do the same?

REVISITING LILY AND WILLY

On our second visit, two years later in May 2012, there was one child more in the gibbon family at the Elmvale Zoo. Once again I was nervous about whether I would see anything to write about. Will there be a story? And what did they call the new baby—Silly, Dilly (like the DQ bar), Tilly, Billy, or Filly? Angie said the baby's name would be Milly (she had a friend by that name). Angie was right. Milly is a blond like her mother, lighter in colour, although I suspect her colouring will darken a little as she matures, so she will look even more like her mother. She is the smallest gibbon I have ever seen, and just a little over a year old. Like her dad, she is a performer. Milly takes chances when she swings through the compound, throwing herself at the rope with little apparent fear. Her agility and speed are amazing. She flings herself to the front of the cage, then dashes side-to-side rapidly in what looks like almost impossible movement. When she is finally still, she purses her lips slightly and softly hoos at me, unasked, unbidden, but much appreciated. "So what do you think of me now?" she seems to say. Milly then turns around, looks over her right shoulder coyly, and heads back for more swinging. I wonder what a gibbon would think of applause.

Chilly is not there. She has been sent to another zoo. In the wild, adolescent gibbons leave home, as you have read, and zoos need to separate them from their nuclear families, too, sometimes within the same zoo, sometimes to help form a gibbon family somewhere else.

Willy hangs back at first, sitting quietly at the back of the cage. Does he miss Chilly? The two were very close two years ago. But then he comes to the front and the family grooming begins. He has been through this experience of the eldest child moving out before, as you'll see in the story about Isabella later in this chapter.

I noticed early the changes that were made in the compound. With intelligent animals such as gibbons (and parrots), you have to change the setup so that they don't get bored. The people who run this zoo clearly understand that important principle.

Talking to veteran keeper Cleo Kelly, I learn from an expert. She's been with gibbons for over 20 years, and her love for them shows. She tells me that juvenile gibbons play blind man's bluff, an old game that kids were still playing when I was young. In the human version, a blindfold is tied around someone's eyes and others dodge back and forth, just out of reach of the "blind man's" outstretched arms. Gibbons aged one to four close their eyes and reach out trying to find the others around them. The anthropologist in me wonders why this game is played—what purpose does this serve? But then I think: swinging high in the trees, you can't always see what is coming up, and fast reaction and adaption are important. Perhaps this helps them learn to do that. Or perhaps it's just (or mostly) fun.

Nicholas and Isabella

Isabella was Willy and Lily's first-born daughter. It appears that Lily was not the good mother with Isabella that she later was with Chilly and then with Milly. She might not have had much of an opportunity to learn how to be a good mother. I don't know enough about her early years to be able to say. Was she raised by humans or by her own mother? In any event, Cleo had to hand-raise young Isabella, who is now seven years old. Nicholas is about the same age, acquired by the zoo when he was about 5½ years old.

They had some adapting to do when they were first placed together in their own compound. They had two separate rooms at first, would visit each other, and then retreat at the end of the day to their own rooms. Gradually, they spent more and more time together. Now the two appear to be inseparable. They also had to learn to groom. I had long thought that since all primates groom each other, grooming was natural, something of an instinct. But perhaps just as much, it is a behavior that needs to be observed, and then learned with a shared intelligence. Cleo was the grooming teacher. She would groom Isabella, and then, eventually, Nicholas wanted to be groomed, too. Gradually, they began to groom each other. Lesson learned. If you don't see it, you don't do it. Imagine trying to swim if you had never seen someone else swim.

When I first saw them, they were two blonds together, hugging almost as though it was a dance routine, each trying to position herself or himself to gain some advantage that I could not see.

I was told that Nicholas was skinny when he first came to the Elmvale Zoo, but began to bulk up. I quickly saw evidence of this when they split up from their long hug. He is big, the biggest non-siamang gibbon I have ever seen. His big shoulders are not all thick hairy fluff, but are buffed up as well. Perhaps they should have called him Arnie instead of Nicholas. I first wondered how he became so powerful. But then, I watched more carefully how he not only swings but whips himself forward, using more muscle than just gravity. His swinging was a true workout.

Isabella is the acrobatic equal of her two sisters Chilly and Milly. She can do some amazing tricks. Once she fell over from a perch backwards, deliberately, and then grabbed the rope, saving her from striking the ground violently. I wonder what happened the first time she tried that move. She did not train with a net to catch her, as human circus acrobats do. It helps to be light and to have soft, thick fur to cushion your fall.

Together they perform a swing chase scene that could fill a gibbon action movie. Moves are sudden, changes of direction quickly executed. Looked at another way, you could say it is like square dancing for apes, ending with a "return to hug" call by the square-dance caller. They follow this up with a mutual hooing session that sounds almost like a basic song duet but without any of the fancy and unique sounds I had heard from Samson and Carmen. Not bad for two zoo-raised gibbon young adults sharing a compound on a warm summer's afternoon.

There is a stuffed gibbon toy in the upper left-hand corner which seems to be more Nicholas's territory than Isabella's. He tends—literally—to hang out there. Isabella picks the stuffed toy up and handles it very much like a human mother would an infant. Eventually she leans it gently up against her shoulder. When it's Nicholas's turn to "practice parent," he slings it over his shoulder and holds it upside down. —Well, he's a guy. Isabella then hangs herself upside down with her feet grasping the rope, whether inspired by Nicolas's bad parenting and as a way to rescue her "child" I cannot say, but it is an impressive move.

While I observed that Nicholas does most of the chasing, Isabella sometimes takes the lead, and she well knows how to take shortcuts that surprise her agile mate. He just escapes in time. Once, one body-checked the other in a rapid change of direction. I don't know whether it was deliberate, but it was a good check. Their ancestors may have come from southeast Asia, but they are definitely Canadian apes, these two. I wonder how gibbons would play hockey. He swings. He scores.

Holding Honey's Hand

It was late in the summer of 2011. Angie and I wanted to take a drive in the country. I chose an area, and looked online to find interesting places to visit there. I found the Northwood Zoo and Animal Sanctuary, a small non-profit zoo that did a lot of rehabilitation work with exotic animals. On the website under the icon "gallery" we saw a picture of a gibbon. So off we went. Both the village of Seagrave and the zoo, located on the edges of the village, were easy to miss, but we eventually found both.

She was alone. It was the first time I had ever seen a gibbon in a zoo that didn't share a cage with another gibbon or a family unit. She was lying on the ground, something I had never seen a gibbon do in a zoo. It would be easy to say that she was lonely. But was she really?

Her neighbour in the next cage was a green monkey (*Chlorocebus sabaeus*), known to be a very sociable species. When the gibbon, a blond white-handed gibbon called Honey, stood up after my wife Angie and I called to her with hoos and short gibbon songs, she went to the side of her compound. So did the green monkey. They groomed each other, taking turns in stretches lasting several minutes. This was clearly a common practice between the two of them. They shared a bond of grooming, primate to primate.

Honey then came to the front of the compound, plastering herself onto the interwoven wires and looking straight at us, but not into our eyes. It is easy, almost always, to say that a gibbon looks lonely; there is ancient Chinese poetry to that effect. But I have found it difficult to tell whether that is generally true. Perhaps it would be more accurate to say that Honey, and others like her, look like "old souls," those human children you meet who look to have experience decades beyond their years. Whatever she felt, I know that gibbons are quite social, so I acted on impulse. I reached out over the fence that stood about a metre away from her compound. I have long, ape-like arms, so I can stretch out a long way for a human. She reached out too, so that I was able to stroke her fingers. They felt rough like those of a farmer or fisherman would. We kept this up until my arm got sore and tired. Reluctantly, I let go. She turned her back to us. Insulted? Insulting? From my experience, I felt neither interpretation was appropriate. She eventually turned around and stretched out her hand to me. I reached through rather than over the fence this time. We could hold hands, and we did, bridging the hundreds of centuries that separated our two species (though fewer hundreds of centuries than separated Honey from her friend the green monkey). It might have been five or ten minutes that we did this, but the experience was unforgettable. Holding Honey's hand was one of my best experiences in researching this book, something never to be forgotten.

Winding the Chapter Up

So now you have met on paper the gibbons I have met in person. And they are persons, people, just shorter, furrier and with proportionately longer arms than humans have. I guarantee that if you go to your local zoo and watch carefully, you will always see a story or stories taking place. Tales are being told in movement and interaction in those compounds. It will not take you long to see that. You could write stories of your own. The more people that do so, the better gibbons will be known. Visit them and record their stories for yourself. You will not be disappointed.

A Gibbon Gallery

Photographs by Angelika Steckley

Above: Tyler and Penelope.

Left: Tyler

Tyler standing tall.

Sandy swinging.

Below: Tyler works out.

Left and below:

Penelope.

Above and to left:

Samson.

Above: John and Penny. Below: John, Penny, and zoo staffer Stefanie.

Above:
Sampson
swinging.

Left: Siamang
in a cage.

Right: Coco
and Giggle.

CHAPTER FIVE
Gibbons I'd Like to Have Met

A
s you can tell from the last chapter, I have been very fortunate in the gibbons that I have met. They have all taught me a lot about the nature and charm of their kind. But I have also read about gibbons that I would like to have met, but haven't. These gibbons have either died or live so far away that it is highly unlikely I will ever get to see them in person. Putting their stories together has been a challenge, but those stories are too important and interesting to ignore. You will learn much from reading about these gibbons, as I learned a great deal in researching and writing about them. There are eight such stories in this chapter: Suzy the siamang; Mary the Müller's gibbon; Bobby Jean, a silvery gibbon; Patzi, an eastern black crested gibbon; Arun Rangsi and Igor, two white-handed gibbons; Toga, a Kloss's gibbon; and Tomoko, possibly a pileated gibbon.

The Maternal Adventures of Suzy the Siamang
Readers were introduced to Suzy (sometimes spelled Susie) the siamang in the 1976 book *The Siamang Gibbons: An Ape Family*, written by children's writer Alice Schick and well-illustrated by her husband, Joel. The focus of the book is primarily on Unk, who would become Suzy's mate. We don't meet up with Suzy until page 43, about halfway through the book. In fact, the first mention of her in the chapter entitled "Suzy" is not until almost at the end of that chapter. She was worth the wait.

Her story, such that I know of it, begins this way. George Speidel, in 1959 the director of the Milwaukee County Zoo, had been looking, unsuccessfully, for a mate for Unk, a seven-year-old male siamang who had fairly recently reached sexual maturity. Then he received a letter from

Seattle, Washington, that was an answer to his (and also perhaps Unk's) dreams: "I have a six-year-old female siamang. . . . Suzy is a beautiful, healthy, gentle animal. I would like nothing better than to find her a mate, so I am willing to sell her to the Milwaukee Zoo."

Suzy had been born and "collected" in the island of Sumatra in western Indonesia, and sent for a short time to a zoo in Seattle. She had been someone's pet for almost her entire six years. And for that reason, her socialization being entirely with humans, the owner felt that she wouldn't make a good mother, not an unreasonable assumption: "I have little hope that Suzy will ever become a mother. She has been raised by humans since she was an infant, and now she thinks she is a human too. I doubt that she will even recognize another siamang as her own kind."

The writer would prove to be wrong, both in questioning Suzy's siamang recognition skills, and her mothering talents and inclinations. She would mother not just siamangs, but the young of other primate species as well.

We are fortunate in having a great deal of information about Suzy provided by the local newspapers in Milwaukee. Unfortunately, even though Suzy and her family were sometimes literally front-page news, the reporters often got their facts wrong. At least twice that I have seen, they overestimated her size (it's the thick fur that made her look "fat"!) and her age. And they kept calling her "it," and not "she" or "her." But that was a product of the times. Scientists typically called apes "it" in the 1960s. Personalizing animals by calling them *she* or *her, he* or *him* was thought to be unscientific, an act of anthropomorphism, defined as inaccurately assuming they had emotions, psychologies and personalities much like our own. One scientist, however, the chimpanzee expert Jane Goodall, led the way in using personal pronouns. She encountered opposition among the male editors of scientific journals:

> The editorial comments on the first paper I wrote for publication demanded that every he or she be replaced with it, and every who be replaced with which. Incensed, I, in my turn, crossed out the its and whichs and scrawled back the original pronouns. As I had no desire to carve a niche for myself in the world of science, but simply wanted to go on living and learning among the chimpanzees, the possible reaction of the editor of the learned journal did not trouble me. In fact I won that round: the paper which finally published did confer upon the chimpanzees the dignity of their

appropriate genders and properly upgraded them from the status of mere 'things' to essential Being-ness.

I wish that she had studied gibbons.

Back to Suzy: she flew from Seattle to Milwaukee (and boy! were her long hairy arms tired!—old joke), arriving in her eventual home on March 31, 1960. According to an article in the *Milwaukee Journal*, headlined "Bride from Sumatra Is Something of an Ape," she stood 3½ feet tall and weighed 35 pounds. More likely she weighed a little less than 25 pounds, a more standard siamang weight. As noted earlier, because of their thick fur, gibbons typically look heavier to uninformed humans than they actually are. The fur is not slimming (unless it is wet, which it usually isn't, as gibbons don't swim, as you may recall).

Now, what about Suzy and Unk and their future together? According to zookeeper Speidel: "The minute he saw her, he got excited. . . . However, she is ignoring him at present. She's tired from her trip."

Their next two meetings in the same cage (her place, not his) were not successful either. Unk was a bit too excited, and a little violent, even though they put him on tranquilizers. That did not work well. The second time they had to hose Unk down. The water would have soaked right into his fur, making him very much like a long-armed walking black sponge.

The third time the two got together in her cage, the zoo people added female hormones (along with the tranquilizers) to the drug cocktail that they gave to the unsuspecting Unk. This seemed to work, although Suzy gave out a little payback, by biting the dopey Unk on the foot. But the two siamangs eventually became a couple, despite the bad beginning of their relationship. It was just like in the old-time movies. Boy meets girl. Boy gets drugged, and girl bites boy in the foot. Boy and girl fall in love.

They didn't mate until the fall of 1961. When Suzy became pregnant, there was some concern about the survival of the child. As far as the zoo staff knew, no siamang baby had ever been successfully born and raised in captivity. This was complicated by the limited "normal" life experiences of the siamang parents. Suzy had been raised by humans, so she had not experienced siamang parenting. The same was true of Unk. And, as you might remember from chapters three and four, siamang fathers play a very active role in parenting little black furry long-armed bundles of joy and energy. He would not have experienced what that was like on the child side. So how could he know what to do on the parent side?

After a gestation period of 230 days (less than eight months), a six-ounce baby girl siamang was born in July 1962. (A full-term human baby of a well-nourished mother weighs about 7½ pounds, 20 times this baby siamang's weight.) The zoo won an award from the American Association of Zoological Parks and Aquariums for the successful breeding of a relatively rare animal. As the zoo staff wisely did not want to approach the parents and child too closely in the compound, they did not know her sex. They called her Mark. She survived to adulthood, and was later moved to another zoo.

One reason for the move was that Suzy and Unk had made life tough for her as an adolescent or sub-adult of about seven. This passage from Alice Schick's book tells the tale:

> During the fall, Mark was placed under increasing stress. Suzy acted hostile toward her, and Mark learned to avoid her mother. Unk's hostility was harder to avoid. Her father began to kick her, hanging from a bar by his hands and swinging his feet into her chest. He sometimes chased her around the enclosure, forcing her to retreat into the shift cage. Three times, he even followed her into the shift cage and continued to attack.

In the abstract to her paper "Some Comparisons between Siamang and Gibbon Behaviour," Greysolynne J. Fox, then a graduate student in anthropology, wrote about Mark's situation: "She was almost never the object of grooming activity and she was allowed to eat only when the family had finished eating. Aggression at feeding time, particularly by the adult male [Unk], was both covert [hidden] and overt."

It is important to note that Unk and Suzy weren't really being bad siamang parents. They were acting to support Mark's younger brother, Smitty, whom we'll meet below. It wasn't favouritism so much as survival of the youngest, a natural siamang parenting practice.

Suzy and Unk's next two offspring died, as infants, of pneumonia. Milwaukee is a lot colder than Indonesia, and siamangs do not have nice warm fur on them when they are first born. They are born naked, just like humans.

The fourth child was born about one month prematurely on May 22, 1967. In an article entitled "Fight for Life," zoo director Speidal told the reporter, "It's pretty much touch and go whether it [he] will live. . . . There's something wrong with its [his] eyes. It [He] can't seem to open them." And he wasn't nursing from his mother. But the little guy survived, and received the name of Smitty, after the newspaper photographer who first took a picture of the young fellow.

Smitty became something of a media star. An article entitled "Smitty the Baby Ape Cuts Apron Strings" appeared in the *Milwaukee Journal* of September 28, 1967. The article celebrated Smitty's first steps away from mom, and possibly towards dad if he was a typical siamang child:

> . . . the first four months of his life have been spent clinging to mother—when she sits, when she lies down or when she swings through the cage.
>
> Now Smitty is learning to walk and he can climb three feet up the pole of a metal climbing rack. He also can hang by one hand.
>
> But he doesn't overdo it. After a few minutes of adventure, he's back with mother again.

He was not the last of Suzy's babies. Les, a younger brother, was born later and survived. Two more babies were born, but did not make it. Sam was the eighth and last. There was a short piece in the *Milwaukee Sentinel* entitled "Siamang Fights for Life at Zoo," in which, calculating the odds from prior births (three survivors out of seven born), Speidel figured that Sam had about a fifty/fifty chance of survival (more accurately 43/57; *Milwaukee Sentinel*, February 7, 1972). Sam beat the odds. He was their last child. Unk received a vasectomy, so he could father no more children.

That is where Suzy's story in *The Siamang Gibbons: An Ape Family* ends. We will continue it from there.

Suzy and Unk continued their assault on the siamangs-in-zoos record book, as they lived into the 1980s. Their big hair would have helped them fit into the rock groups of the era. As the two were in their thirties, they were considered old by the standards of siamangs living in zoos or the wild. And their relationship extended over 25 years. They were a close couple. Even after all that time together, they did not like to be separated from each other for long. An article in the *Milwaukee Journal* dated February 11, 1985, reported that "often, after Unk and Suzie are apart for a while, they quickly run to each other and give one another big hugs." That, of course, is the recognition hug we talked about in the last chapter. However, it was around that time that Unk developed diabetes, and needed regular insulin shots to combat it. In 1988, he died from the disease.

Suzy continued on, but not alone. In 1991, she would receive more media attention. She would help with a situation with which she was familiar. There was a young primate mother, seven years old, who had been raised by humans, and so was not thought to be able to mother her newborn well. In this case, unlike that of Suzy years ago, it was not merely suspected, but proved to be true. The young mother neither fed nor cuddled her two-month-old son.

Suzy came to the rescue. What makes this case particularly interesting is that the baby was not a siamang, nor any species of gibbon, nor even an ape. He was a spider monkey, a species that lives in the wilds of Central and South America, far from the Asian lands in which gibbons swing wild. While the keepers fed the young fellow, Suzy took to him immediately and provided the appropriate maternal care. She would foster mother this lucky young monkey for almost two years, from August 5, 1991 to May 4, 1993. He was then sent to a zoo in Detroit.

Later that same year, at the grand siamang age of 41, she performed the same feat again, but with her own species. On September 13, 1993, a female siamang named Jocoma was born in the Houston Zoological Gardens. Her mother had given birth through caesarean section, like Penelope's mom in the last chapter. And also like Penelope's mom, she was unwilling, and perhaps physically unable, to take care of her infant daughter. Jocoma was for the first almost three months of her life raised by humans with the help of a gorilla plush toy as a stand-in mother to hold on to.

Too bad it wasn't a gibbon plush toy, but as my wife Angie and I can attest, they are not often available in stores or zoo gift shops.

Having lost her mate and her most recent child, Suzy was described as being "inactive and uninterested" in life at that time. She might have been suffering from empty nest syndrome (which human parents experience when their children finally leave the house for good), but, if you remember from chapter two, gibbons, unlike the larger apes, do not build nests. What did she need to be happy? In an article published in 1993, the curator of the primates noted that "at what time Suzy got ahold of Jocoma, her eyes brightened up. . . . Now it's all new again."

The bonding was not just one way. Jocoma would soon learn the baby gibbon joys of what it was like to be held constantly. Reportedly, "Suzy wasn't about to let her go." This even included those scary times when mom would be swinging up high at the top of the compound. Remembering well what it felt like the one (and only) time I flew in a small plane piloted by my Uncle Sandy Lawson, I can relate.

Suzy's fostering was a success. Jocoma was able to leave as a healthy, stable siamang in the spring of 1995 to join the animals at the Memphis Zoo. She lived there for a little over 15 years.

After Jocoma and over the course of the next year, Suzy would foster two more baby siamangs, from the Brookfield Zoo in Chicago. They stayed in the compound next door. Suzy was engaged in maternal multitasking.

In April, 1994, Suzy the mothering marvel died of complication from the flu. She picked the disease up from her foster children. She was about 52 years old and had lived a full life.

Mary, Mary, Wild and Scary

Mary, a Müller's gibbon, was the acknowledged but unofficial queen of the Taronga Zoo in Sydney, Australia. Despite the fact that she weighed only about 12 pounds (that's about average for an adult Müller's gibbon, male or female), there are many people and zoo animals who visited or lived in that zoo who would have called her scary. And that wasn't just because that word rhymes so easily with Mary.

She had a difficult start to life. She was captured as an infant in her native island of Borneo in the South Pacific. She ended up not long afterward in Australia in December of 1960.

She was no Suzy the Siamang. Motherhood did not work well for her. It doesn't for everyone, whether gibbon or human. Mary and Robinson, her mate, had eight children. None of them survived for long, for reasons I have not read about. She had her Fallopian tubes tied in 1982, so she could not give birth to any more little gibbon babies that probably would not survive.

After Robinson died in 1986, the keepers at the zoo tried to pair her off with Silver, a much older male Müller's gibbon. To keep them "chilled" during their first days together, the staff gave Mary and Silver each five milligrams of the anti-anxiety medication Valium each day (the usual human dose is 2 to 10 milligrams, twice to four times a day). The plan didn't work. She just didn't seem to like being with him.

And she would let him know how she felt. There are two different versions of a story about Silver and the moat that surrounded their compound. Both of them make Mary seem scary. You might remember from the second chapter that gibbons do not swim. That is why gibbon compounds in zoos often have a moat separating gibbon territory from human territory. That is the way it is at the Taronga Zoo. The map of the zoo has a small figure of a gibbon hanging in the typical position, with an island of green in the middle of a tiny body of water in light blue.

One version of the story states that Silver could not stand being with Scary Mary, and decided to take a long leap into the moat to escape. He is said to have emerged at the other side, wet but safe, sopping but surviving Mary-free. The other version says that one day, wanting to get rid of Silver, Mary just pushed him into the water. Either way, her reputation grew as hard to live with. The zoo did not try in the future to pair her with anyone new.

There might be a third version of the story, depicted in two works of art composed in 2011 by Hobart Hughes, and represented on the Taronga Zoo website. One is an ink-and-pencil drawing. At first you just see a gibbon in a typical pose, hanging from a branch. But if you look closely, and look up, you see another gibbon biting "his" (I think the first one is male) right hand. I'll bet that second gibbon is Mary. Then there is a piece of ceramic artwork that depicts what looks to me like a gibbon falling in the water, with splashes all around him. The gender of that gibbon is not clear, but if it fits with the other then it would seem to be Mary's male victim.

Mary had her own scary experience with the moat. One year, a nasty tropical storm hit the zoo. When the skies finally cleared, members of the zoo staff were shocked to see that a tree that had been standing in the middle of Mary's compound had blown down into the water. Looking for the little primate, expecting to see her body lying motionless on land or in the moat, floating but not moving, they found nothing. They noticed that the tree had formed a bridge. She must have escaped. Where did she go? Where could she go? According to the public relations chief who wrote about her Taronga Zoo experiences:

> Mary ran straight into the secure arms of her keeper Paul Davies, grateful to see a friendly face after such a terrible ordeal. I think it must have the first and last time that Mary has ever been pleasant to the keepers. She still mutters ungratefully at them every time they clean out her house.

I have several times heard from zoo workers that one of the delights of working at a zoo with gibbons is the early morning singing of the small apes. Darill Clements, in her book *Postcards from the Zoo: Animal Tales from a 25-Year Zoo Safari*, wanted to feature gibbon singing on the occasion of the seventieth anniversary of the Taronga Zoo during a live radio broadcast from a location beside Mary's compound. But no sweet, enchanting gibbon songs were heard that morning. Mary had a special silent statement to make. Clements looked over at the compound and saw Mary. "As I took a closer look," Clements recalled, "I realised it wasn't her quaint old face she was showing us—it was her dark and hairy backside that she was pointing in our direction. We had obviously disturbed her beauty sleep and she was not amused." Too bad it hadn't been a local television station that had come to record Mary's song. The video would have gone viral. And for the purposes of poetry, it is too bad that gibbon does not rhyme with moon.

Mary died on February 13, 2015, aged 57. Until very late in life, she remained strong, sitting on top of her fig tree looking down upon the lesser creatures beneath her, human and non-human—her subjects. Mary was a solo singer, her distinctive song one of the welcome sounds of her zoo. She had a bit of arthritis in her ankles and wrists, but she still moved around well. And apart from observing others and eating, her greatest joy was to be groomed by her keepers. When you are a queen, even a scary one, you get to enjoy that type of special treatment. And apparently there was a new coconut-oil concoction in her food that kept her skin from getting dry, and her from looking her age, not that she was looking for a mate.

Arun Rangsi: The Number that Gained a Name

A baby boy white-handed gibbon was born August 9, 1979, at the Comparative Oncology Laboratory at the University of California, Davis. It was a horrible place for him to begin life. Six days later, he was found lying on the floor of his cage, with what were termed by the lab people "multiple abrasions over his body." Apparently, he had been dropped and abandoned by his mother. But what were the chances that she could be a good parent? She was a lab gibbon too. She had been imported in 1973 to be experimented on at the deadly cancer laboratory from the U.S.-controlled captive lab-gibbon colony in Bangkok, Thailand, a place where the unfortunate animals "had been used in many experiments involving the inoculation of blood from two Thai malaria patients, spleen removal, infection with dengue fever, and exposure to herpes virus."

The director of the California lab received research funding from the National Cancer Institute to do similar work from 1972 to 1980. He built up his own lab-gibbon colony by various means, both legal and illegal. He did not seem to care how he got his disposable primates. And disposable they were. Young gibbons were inoculated with material obtained from gibbons dying of experimentally induced cancer, and with a virus suspected of causing cancer.

After being rejected by his mother, the infant male gibbon was put in a separate cage that contained a metal mother, made of wire and covered with cloth. A famous and somewhat heartless experiment performed by psychologist Harry Harlow on baby rhesus monkeys around that time had shown that monkeys raised with these metal mothers were a little more emotionally healthy than those put into empty cages. But I would say it wasn't much of an improvement. I wonder what kind of childhood Harlow had.

The young gibbon was never given a name at the lab, but at four months of age was blue-tattooed with number HL-98, so the experimenters would know who he was in an impersonal kind of way. In the course of experiments, he twice contracted both pneumonia and bacillary dysentery (a disease often fatal in young primates), and suddenly lost 10% to 20% of his body weight. He did not have a lot of weight to lose to begin with. In August 1980, when he was one year old, his weight dropped from 1.2 kilograms to 1.05 kilograms, or barely 2.3 pounds.

He wasn't emotionally healthy either. A sign of the stress that he was undergoing was a large callus above his right ear. It was caused by his constantly banging his head against glass windows, walls, anything that potentially offered itself as an object suitable for head-banging.

And his gibbon skills weren't developing normally either. Even when approaching two years of age, he could not swing or run like a normal gibbon youngster.

Then the lab fell on hard times. In 1976, with the designation of gibbons as endangered species, the lab director had to get a special U.S. federal license to obtain gibbons for research. Then the lab lost its federal funding, and had to relocate its gibbons.

Enter Shirley McGreal and her International Protection of Primates League (IPPL). They negotiated a deal with the reluctant lab director to relocate the little guy in South Carolina, where the IPPL had its sanctuary. To do this, they had to get approval from the U.S. Fish and Wildlife Service. These were the same people who, not too long before, had given the lab permission to kill ten infant gibbons a year in the name of medical research.

One reason why the young gibbon was allowed to leave was because the lab director claimed that the little fellow was "mentally retarded" and "metabolically abnormal," and highly unlikely to be able to breed.

Then HL-98's big travel adventure began. He was collected by Christine Saup of the Animal Protection Institute on August 8, 1981. She drove him 100 miles, the farthest he had ever travelled, to catch a plane bound from San Francisco to Atlanta, Georgia. Charleston, South Carolina was relatively close to the IPPL sanctuary, but that would involve a transfer of planes. There was a big air traffic controllers' strike on then; airports were disorganized. McGreal was worried that the little gibbon might get lost in the transfer, like checked luggage, only alive and furry. So she and a friend drove 300 miles for five hours through a "rainy night in Georgia" (the name of a popular song from a few years before) to pick him up and drive him to the sanctuary. That is serious dedication to gibbon rescue.

The plane landed safely, but the rescuers felt some concern about whether the young gibbon was actually aboard. When the pilot was asked whether there was a gibbon on board the plane, he responded with "No, but we do have a chimpanzee," referring to what was written on the shipping manifest. Trusting in the invisibility of gibbons and the general ignorance of people concerning their existence (i.e., if it is a relatively small ape it *must* be a chimpanzee, because it is too small to be a gorilla or orangutan), they asked for the chimpanzee. They waited in deep concern for 20 long minutes for the sky kennel carrying the young ape to arrive. Would that be him? Would the little fellow be alive?

When the kennel arrived, they saw the young gibbon, nothing more than a little brown bundle of fur. He was small for his age, weighing only four pounds at this point. His face was pink, not the usual darker brown of other gibbons, as he had never been exposed to the sun. Gibbons tan, and in my experience they appear to like to lie in the sun.

Even after they took him home to the sanctuary, he still banged his head. A psychologist suggested to McGreal that she bang her head too, hoping that would help him stop the practice. The somewhat bizarre therapy worked. Don't try that at home without a helmet.

They had to give him a name. A number was not enough for the increasingly lively bundle of gibbon they were learning to love. He received the name "Arun Rangsi," a Thai Buddhist term meaning "The Rising Sun of Dawn," a good name to symbolize the new beginning he had just been given.

How would he react to other gibbons? That might have been a problem. He had probably never been given the chance to freely interact with someone of his own kind before. But he responded well when two other gibbons, Helen and Peppy, came to the sanctuary a year later.

And what about a mate? Eventually he was introduced to a female, also a former lab gibbon, who had been named "Lost" by the lab people. She was renamed the more fitting "Shianti," a word in Sanskrit (the sacred language of Hinduism and Buddhism) meaning "Peace." The name suited her, as she was a relatively laid back, certainly in contrast to the hyperactive Arun Rangsi.

There was some concern as to how he would be as a father, as he hadn't been properly parented himself. There was no need for that concern, as he became a good gibbon father.

In 2011, there was a celebration at IPPL, honouring the 30 years that Arun Rangsi had been at the sanctuary. He was and is a success story for the sanctuary that gave him a home.

Igor: A Long Happy Ending

If you like stories with a happy ending, you will really like Igor's story. It does not start happily, however. As a baby white-handed gibbon, he was captured in the wilds of Thailand, his mother probably shot and killed, a standard and incredibly hideous way of obtaining baby gibbons that I discuss in the next chapter. This took place sometime around 1956. He was sold to a drug company in the United States while he was still an infant. For five years they conducted experiments on him, and then sold him to another lab, this one affiliated with New York University. It was called the New York Laboratory for Experimental Medicine and Surgery in Primates (LEMSIP). There he lived a sad life for 21 years. His "home" was a cage covered with black Plexiglas in a windowless trailer. He was not alone in the sense that there were other gibbons nearby, enslaved in the same situation, but he was certainly lonely. He could not see the others, just hear them.

Not being properly raised, by gibbons or humans, he did not know how to react to his own species. In fact, when he saw another gibbon, he reacted by savagely tearing at his arms with his teeth. This self-mutilation was his response to his oppressive situation.

As he matured to a middle-aged gibbon in his thirties, he got a chance at freedom. One of the veterinarians responsible for taking care of the lab gibbons initiated actions that led to four of their number being sent to a sanctuary run by the International Primate Protection League.

Igor was sent there in June 1987; he was free at last. But how could they take care of him? He was a psychologically scarred animal, and those scars would last beyond the time it took his arms to physically heal.

Having taken in rescue dogs and one very biting-prone rescue Senegal parrot called Sam, I know the difficulties of raising and taking care of such an animal.

Initially, they kept the other gibbons at the sanctuary out of his sight, but not out of his hearing. That seemed to work. He did not bite himself when he heard their sounds. He also liked the sights and sounds of the local wildlife, birds and squirrels. And he took well to the company of dogs.

Then in 2002, Courtney was born, a young, hairless female. Feeling that she would pose no threat, they had her visit him once a week, carrying her in and putting the two of them under careful supervision. It worked. He enjoyed those visits, and continued to do so for six years, until she got too big to bring in in that way.

Then there was Michael, another bachelor gibbon. His compound was within visual range of his black furred, white faced neighbour, even though Igor didn't have the best vision (he had cataracts). Seeing Michael did not seem to cause Igor to react with self-mutilation or any other psychologically abnormal behaviour. Instead, he seemed glad of the company.

When Michael moved out, it was time for Gibby. He added a vocal dimension to the relationship. The two gibbons would sing to each other, tying bonds like long extension cords between their two separated compounds.

Igor passed away following a severe stroke on October 13, 2014. He was 58, extremely elderly by gibbon standards. But in July, 2012, Igor and the IPPL had celebrated his silver anniversary as a happy, free gibbon. There is your happy ending.

Bobby-Jean: Mother of All Silvery Gibbons

In chapter two you read about how the silvery or Javan gibbon is endangered, with perhaps 2,000 individuals remaining.

This is the story of Bobby-Jean, whose family is doing their best to keep the species from becoming extinct. She was captured in 1958 on the island of Java, Indonesia. In 1964 she arrived, with three other gibbons, at Assiniboine Park Zoo in Winnipeg, Manitoba, having been bought from a dealer in the Netherlands. There were chains around the gibbons' necks as they arrived in Winnipeg, soon to be removed once they came to the sanctuary of this gibbon-friendly zoo.

Bobby-Jean soon became a much-loved character at that zoo. One of her tricks was to observe visitors by using a mirror. She would turn her back on the humans who would approach her cage, and place the mirror so that she could still see them, without their being able to see her face. In the words of keeper Bob Wrigley:

> I was amazed one day to watch Bobby-Jean watching the public with her mirror. She had her back to the public and she was watching people's expressions over her shoulder and I thought, "My gosh, there's a lot going on in that little head of hers."

Her use of the mirror is scientifically interesting as the ability to recognize yourself in a mirror is considered a sign of intelligence. It is an ability that a relatively few smart animals (e.g., the larger apes, elephants and crows) are reckoned by some scientists to possess. I believe that at least one of our parrots, Lime, a yellow-headed Amazon, has this ability. She can be easily provoked, but she does not attack the bathroom mirror when I am brushing my teeth with her on my right shoulder. She just cocks her head.

A recent study claims to have demonstrated that gibbons did not pass this test. In the experiment, an animal subject has a mark put on his or her face, a mark visible only through seeing it in the mirror. If the subject shows recognition of the fact that it is herself or himself in the mirror, typically by trying to brush off the mark, then the subject is judged by the people in white lab coats to have exhibited a kind of self-recognition. The gibbons tested did not show such signs of recognition, even though they were deemed as being "highly motivated" to find the mark. The motivation supposedly came from the fact that the gibbons were marked with icing that they had previously gobbled up when it was put in front of them. Maybe it would have been better just to put the mirror in the compound where the gibbons were living, giving them time to figure out how to use it. That seems to have worked with Bobby-Jean. Wouldn't you perform better on an intelligence test or any other test if you were given more time to experiment and think things through? I question the validity of the test.

I would like to watch Samson, the white-handed gibbon resident in Jungle Cat World, to see his reaction to the mirror that is sometimes hung in his cage. Apparently, it is one of his favourite toys. The way that he can strike a pose makes me think that he knows the "man (gibbon) in the mirror."

BOBBY-JEAN AS A MOTHER

Bobby-Jean's first experience with childbirth was sad. Not only did her baby die the day she was born (March 3, 1966), but Bobby-Jean's first mate also died that same month. Then came Billy-Joe (I'm so glad that the humans that named them did not call their children Billy-Jean and Bobby-Joe, or I would never get the names right).

Billy-Joe was born in Java in 1959. The two B-J's produced 11 silvery gibbon babies. Remarkably, eight of their children survived past their first birthdays. These children, their grandchildren, great-grandchildren and even at least one great-great-grandchild are in zoos all over the world: in Australia, England, France, Germany, Northern Ireland and the United States. They are favourites for breeding loans, where the home zoos own the loaned parent and some of the offspring, but the rest of the children go to the borrowing zoo.

Bobby-Jean died, roughly 50 years old, in December, 2007, the oldest recorded age of any Javan gibbon known. Her contribution to the world continues, as you will see.

ASSINI: A DAUGHTER CARRIES ON THE FAMILY LINE

The name "Assini" is based on the word for "stone" used by the Cree, a people who live in northern Quebec, Ontario, Manitoba, Saskatchewan and Alberta. The word is found in the name of the zoo where she was born, Assiniboine, which means "cooking with stones" in Cree. Assini was born in 1980, the fifth child of Bobby-Jean and Billy-Joe. She was initially named Jasmine (and this was 12 years before the Disney movie *Aladdin*), but fortunately the name was changed to something more unusual, something Canadian.

Assini was transferred to Howletts Wild Animal Park in England in 1989. There she and her mate Omar (born in the wild in Java, possibly in 1984) would be as prolific as her parents were. They produced eight daughters and two sons. In 2006, they would be on breeding loan to the Belfast Zoo, taking with them daughter Dieng (born in 2002) and son Wayang (born in 2004), both named after mountains in Java. In 2007, Belle, a girl, was born, and in 2009, Haja, their tenth child, came into this world, but died shortly after her birth.

Dieng would get to travel again, this time much farther away, to the Fort Wayne Zoo in Indiana. In 2011, she and her mate Lionel (more about him below) produced Jaka, whose name is an Indonesian word meaning "young man." According to the Fort Wayne Zoo's website, it is the only zoo in North America to exhibit Javan gibbons.

One of Assini's daughters, Yoni, would stay at Howletts and with her mate, born in Munich, Germany, would give birth to four children. One of them, their son Anak (born in 1999), himself fathered a child in 2005.

Another daughter, Kulon, would remain at Howletts, where, with a Munich-born male, she would have two children. One of them, a daughter named Layar (born 2002), was loaned out to the Mogo Zoo in south-eastern Australia. In 2010, their website featured a picture of her with her infant daughter Cinta (born in June 2009), Bobby-Jean's first great-great-grandchild, surely with more to come.

HECLA AND HER DESCENDANTS

Hecla, Bobby-Jean and Billy-Joe's sixth child, was born in 1983. In 1992, she was loaned out to the Perth Zoo in western Australia. There, with her mate Jury (from Tierpark Berlin), she has had five offspring: Khusus, Regina, Arjuna, Sinta and Nakula, with four surviving beyond a year old. Daughter Khusus, born in 1995, was loaned out in 2000 by the Assini-boine Park Zoo to the Gibbon Conservation Center in California (GCC), where with old-timer (30 years old) Ushko she had by 2012 given birth to two children. Daughter Regina is well-travelled, and in the near future will take another long trip—back to the large island where her grandmother was born. She was born in Perth, Australia, in 1998, and loaned to the Taronga Zoo in Sydney in 2004. In 2010, she travelled over 10,000 miles to the Port Lympne Zoo in southeastern England, where they initially hoped she would breed. But there had been a change in plans. As part of an effort to raise the wild silvery gibbon population in Java, in 2012 that zoo returned Regina, as well as some Javan langurs (monkeys of the genus *Semnopithecus*), to the Indonesian island. At the end of September 2014, she was released into the wild.

Chloe, Bobby-Jean's eighth child, was born in 1990. She was also loaned out by the Assiniboine Park Zoo to the GCC in California. There she produced five children. Her mate is Shelby, himself on breeding loan from Perth. The third child, Lionel, was born in 2001. As noted above, he is now Dieng's mate. Between Chloe and her sister Khusus, they have given birth to all seven of the silvery gibbons born in the United States.

Bobby-Jean and her descendants have certainly done their bit to fight off the extinction of the silvery gibbon. To help you keep straight who is who, check out the following table.

List of Bobby-Jean's Family Members Mentioned

First Couple	Bobby-Jean (1958), Billy-Joe (1959)
Their Children	Assini (1980), Hecla (1983), Chloe (1990)
Assini and Omar's (1984) Children (Bobby-Jean's Grandchildren)	Yoni, Kulon, Reggat, Pangrango (1997), Cisolok, Dieng (2002), Wayang (2004), Belle (2007), Haja (2009)
Yoni's Child (Bobby-Jean's Great-Grandchild)	Anak (1999)
Kulon's Child (Bobby-Jean's Great-Grandchild)	Layar (2002)
Layar's Child (Bobby-Jean's Great-Great-Grand-child)	Cinta (2009)
Pangrango's Children (Bobby Jean's Great-Grandchildren)	Flip (2005), Isabel (2008), Kim (2010)
Dieng's Child (Bobby-Jean's Great-Grandchild)	Jaka
Hecla's Children (Bobby-Jean's Grandchildren)	Khusus (1995), Regina (1998), Arjuna, Sinta, Nakula (2005)
Chloe's Child (Bobby-Jean's Grandchild)	Lionel

Zoos and Other Organizations Involved with Bobby-Jean's Family

Organization	Country	Identification
Assiniboine Park Zoo	Canada	Bobby-Jean's home
Howletts Wild Animal Park	England	Assini's home
Belfast Zoo	Northern Ireland	Assini sent on loan to
Fort Wayne Zoo	United States	Dieng's home
Mogo Zoo	Australia	Layar's home
Perth Zoo	Australia	Hecla sent on loan to
Gibbon Conservation Center	United States	Khusus sent on loan to
Port Lympne Zoo	England	Regina's home
Munich Zoo	Germany	Pangrango sent on loan to
St.-Martin-La-Plaine	France	Cisolok sent on loan to

In short—though maybe this comes too late after listing all those names!—if you see a Javan gibbon in a zoo anywhere in the world, it is a fairly safe bet that swinging through the compound is at least one individual carrying the genes of Bobby-Jean.

Patzi: The Postcard Gibbon

Patzi is kind of a cover girl gibbon. But the cover she appeared on was one side of a zoo postcard. Patzi was a *Nomascus nasutus*, otherwise known as the Cao Vit or eastern black-crested gibbon. If you remember Chapter Three (but no, this is not a test!), you might recall that her species lives in the border area of Vietnam and southern China. Their adult colouring is distinctive to each sex. Males are basically black, while the females are typically a beautiful golden colour. Some individuals, however, do not perfectly fit into this colour pattern. Patzi would seem to have been one of those. That is why she was not identified as a Cao Vit gibbon during her lifetime. She was considered to be "too black" to be a Cao Vit. She had a broad black stripe running from the top of her head down to the middle of her stomach, looking very much like a black bib, although no bibs I have ever seen connect with the top of the head.

As far as we know, she was born in the wild in northeastern Vietnam. German scientist Wolfgang Fischer travelled in September 1962 to Hanoi, capital of what was then called North Vietnam, to purchase her for Tierpark Berlin, where he had the job of Inspector of Animals. She arrived there in November of the same year. At that time, the zoo had been in operation for less than 10 years. Now it is considered the largest zoo in Europe. As someone who grew up during the 1960s, I at first found it somewhat strange that someone who appeared to have been a western scientist could have travelled to North Vietnam at that time. There was a war going on between the north and south parts of Vietnam, with communist countries supporting the north and capitalist countries (mainly the United States) supporting the south. But in fact the park was in what was then *East* Berlin, located in what was then called East Germany (before the reunification in 1990 of West and East Germany into one country). East Germany was part of what was called the Soviet bloc, dominated by the communist USSR.

It was thought that Patzi was an infant about 12 to 16 months old when she arrived in East Germany in November 1962. By 1964, her picture started appearing on postcards, a rare case of gibbon visibility in Europe. In fact, her face became one of the most identifiable in the entire zoo. Fischer wrote a short, 39-page-long book, *Das Jahr mit den Gibbons* (roughly translated as *The Year with the Gibbons*), that was published in 1966, and articles in 1980 and 1981, all of which provided his detailed observations of how Patzi developed, both physically and in terms of behaviour.

She lived in Tierpark Berlin zoo until her death at roughly 24 in 1986. At that time she was considered a *Hylobates concolor*, the concolor or black-crested gibbon (without the adjective "eastern" attached), which is a different species. In 1989, biologist and gibbon guru Thomas Geissmann studied her remains, and compared them with the remains and living bodies of several kinds of closely related gibbons. He believed at that time that she was a *Nomascus hainanus*, or Hainan black-crested gibbon. But today she is generally recognized as the most famous example of a nearly extinct species, *Nomascus nasutus*, although there is not yet unanimous agreement on whether this is what she was.

There should be more gibbons on postcards, with perhaps a little text explaining that they are not monkeys because they don't have tails.

Toga: The Gibbon Who Feared Heights

Can you imagine a gibbon fearing heights? That would be like a bee fearing crowds, or a crocodile being afraid of mud. The story of such a gibbon begins and ends on the island of Siberut, off the west coast of Sumatra, Indonesia. It is the story of a Kloss's gibbon who was one of the gibbons featured in Anthony Whitten's excellent book, *The Gibbons of Siberut* (1982).

One day, Tony and his wife Jane (a good jungle name as you will know if you are familiar with the story of Tarzan) encountered a local man asking for medicine from the western scientist. Somewhat casually, the man mentioned that he had in his possession a baby *beelow* (the local name for gibbon, easy to remember as everything in the jungle is *below* a gibbon), whose mother he had shot and killed. In the vividly descriptive writing that makes Whitten's book such a joy to read, he depicts the first meeting with the gibbon:

> Sure enough, clinging to a chicken basket was a spidery, black furry mass. It squeaked as we approached and held onto its basket for dear life. . . . Jane put her finger in the infant's tiny hand and lifted it to her. Its face formed a deeply furrowed frown and it yelled like a beast possessed until it made contact with her body.

Judging by her lack of tooth development, small size—Tony said she looked like a "furry crayfish," a brilliant description—and immature behaviour, they reckoned that the little gibbon was about 5½ months old. When Tony and Jane returned to camp, the locals joked about her being their first baby. They referred to the furry infant as "togara," meaning "their child." The name was shortened to Toga.

Toga bonded primarily with Tony, as he carried her almost non-stop for the first five days of their travelling. She was daddy's girl. When it rained, she would cling to his chest to try to keep herself as dry as possible. Their close bond could be seen when he returned to camp after going out to do research without her:

> As I approached the camp clearing I heard Toga start to yell, and by the time I reached the veranda she was crawling clumsily out to meet me. I picked her up and she snuggled into my arms, heaving huge sighs of relief. "I don't know how she knows it's you coming out of the forest," Jane said from inside the house. "She never acts the same way when . . . one of the neighbours comes visiting."

As a good foster parent for the young gibbon, Tony wanted her to develop proper gibbon skills. Climbing, swinging, and being comfortable with heights were high (literally!) on the list. One day, he climbed a fruit tree, carrying her on his head. I can relate to the experience, as I often walk around our house with Lime, a yellow-headed Amazon parrot, on my head. When Tony reached a branch about 20 feet off the ground, he stopped and set Toga down on the branch alongside him. He hoped that she would then "gibbon about" in the tree. She didn't. In fact—

> . . . she buried her face in my shirt and clung on in sheer terror. What rotten luck to have an acrophobic [height fearing] gibbon! Now and again she'd twist her head very slowly and then, equally slowly, peer down. But as soon as she saw that the ground had come no closer, she buried her face again and whimpered. Toga still had a long way to go.

Tony and Jane would have Toga for seven months, when unfortunately she died of an unknown illness. And, although Whitten's career as a wild-life biologist later led to his writing books and articles about birds, reptiles, fish, snails and insects, he would not bond with them as he had with young Toga. Carrying a snail on your head is not a lot like having a furry long-limbed little gibbon as headgear. Not that I've had either ex-perience. . . .

Are You Ready for Love, Tomoko?
The Story of a Cambodian Gibbon

The book *Are You Ready for Love, Tomoko?* was composed with much love by author Meenakshi Negi Dufault. It is a highly original work, written from the gibbon Tomoko's imagined first-person point of view (that is, as "I" and "me"). As the gibbon lived in Cambodia, I at first assumed that she was a *Nomascus gabriellae*. However, judging from her pictures, I am now guessing that she was a pileated gibbon. Sometimes I wish they wore labels or stickers saying "Hi, I'm a female pileated gibbon."

Her first life tragedy was one that you, the reader, are probably beginning to become quite familiar with. Her mother was shot and killed. Tomoko and another young female were put in a sack and carried into a local village. From there the two small apes were driven to the big city of Phnom Penh, where they were purchased by people who dealt (both legally and illegally) in the selling of live animals. The place where this diverse and over-crowded animal population was housed was described in dirty detail by the author:

> Box upon box, netted and barred to prevent escape [and] piled atop each other, animals from the forest sat caged. Wild cats, mongoose [weasel-like animals], ducks, roosters, pythons, birds of all colours, parrots, majestic eagles, bears, leopard cubs, dogs of many types and faces, monkeys, monitor lizards, wild rodents, rabbits, exotic animals with depleting populations. . . .
>
> Some to end up as caged pets to be shown off or forgotten and others as exotic meat in Chinese restaurants.
>
> Each creature singularly or in company found itself in a box assigned as his home. Most of these boxes had enough space to stretch only one limb at a time. Pythons seemed to be confused in their winding cycle and lay still, playing dead.

Dufault, along with her husband a foreigner to the country in which they ran a restaurant, came to that outdoor animal warehouse looking merely to purchase a guard dog. Unable to resist the charms of the young primate (Angie and I know how that feels), she left with tiny Tomoko and no dog. The Dufaults raised the young gibbon, with only a few relatively minor biting incidents, until she became strong and full-sized, reaching a healthy six kilograms (a little over 13 pounds). Once she reached maturity, they found her a mate, Sambo, who had his own sad story.

Sambo, too, had been captured as an infant. He first became a farmer's pet, then an object for sale in a portable (motorbike) pet shop, and finally a city family's abused pet. As you will have gathered by now, gibbons are quite intelligent. Sambo managed to undo a latch to escape from his cursed captivity. Starving, fearful and dehydrated, Sambo collapsed. He was found and taken in by a family who knew someone with a monkey and a gibbon. That person took him in for a short time, and then called Dufault.

The two gibbons were not together long before they were flown and bused (accompanied by their owner and along with a number of other gibbons and some monkeys) to a release/rehabilitation camp in the Cambodian province of Siem Reap. The camp was run by the Angkor Center for Conservation of Biodiversity. The author had sound practical reasons for taking Tomoko and Sambo there. When gibbons mature, their adult teeth are large, and they can wound unwary humans. One of the author's two maids had been seriously bitten already.

Sadly, after the passage of only a few months, Tomoko had to be euthanized, or "put down." Having had to put down a much-loved dog, cat, and parrot, as well as a wounded baby raccoon that we had gotten to know and care for in a little over an hour, Angie and I know the pain that comes with that decision. Tomoko had contracted a deadly disorder, one that she may have carried for some years. She was eight years old, a young gibbon adult.

Dufault was devastated, ending the acknowledgements that concluded her book this way: "Finally to Tomoko who brought me much joy and sorrow. Joy in the bonding and crossing over the species and sorrow in the knowledge that she was from the wild and that is where she must return."

Crossing the species barrier is something familiar to most of us who have dog, cat, bird and reptile companions. When the border-crossing involves wild creatures that you are forced to give up, the experience evokes a different set of emotional challenges. Still, they are challenges that add meaning to life.

Leading to the Next Chapter
In this chapter, like the previous one, you have read the stories of gibbons who came to live in zoos or sanctuaries. Some were born in the wild, some in a domesticated setting. A good number were rescued from bad situations in the keeping of humans. Their stories help us understand the nature and intelligence of gibbons, and the possibility of bonds formed

between humans and gibbons. But these domesticated settings cannot serve as the basis for the future survival of the four gibbon genera and their various species. That must be in the wild. That is where their survival is threatened. In the next chapter we will discuss those threats.

CHAPTER SIX
The Endangered Status of Gibbons

T
he most unfortunate aspect about the invisibility of gibbons is that someday these wonderful creatures may really *be* invisible. Sometime in the future gibbons may exist only in pictures, poetry and memories. In other words, some or all species of gibbons may become extinct. All 17 gibbon species are endangered, some extremely so. As we have seen, there are said to be only 17 remaining Hainan black-crested gibbons (*Nomascus hainanus*), living on an island off the coast of China. Matters are little better for the closely related species, the eastern black-crested gibbon *(Nomascus nasutus)*, of which there may now be no more than 50 remaining individuals. These two species may have already passed the point of no return on the long, lonely trail to extinction.

Making the Red List: Not Where You Want Your Name to Be
The International Union for the Conservation of Nature (IUCN) each year publishes a "Red List" of plants and animals that are threatened with possible extinction. The Union has put together a three-part scale, ranging from "critical"—species in imminent threat of extinction—through "endangered" to "vulnerable." A good way of remembering the differences between the rankings is by looking at the first letter in each word. The earlier in the alphabet the letter occurs, the greater the threat. But keep in mind that even "vulnerable" is still not a good place to be when your chances of surviving are being ranked. After all, would you like to be vulnerable to anything—especially if it's extinction?

With that in mind, here are all 17 gibbon species with their status as of 2014 listed:

Species of Gibbons and Their Conservation Status

Genus	Species	Common Names	Conservation Status
Hylobates	lar	White-handed or common	Endangered
	agilis	Agile or black-handed	Endangered
	albibarbis	White-bearded	Endangered
	muelleri	Müller's or grey	Endangered
	moloch	Silvery	Endangered
	pileatus	Pileated or capped	Endangered
	klossi	Kloss's or Mentawi	Endangered
Hoolock	hoolock	Western hoolock	Endangered
	leuconedys	Eastern hoolock	Vulnerable
Symphalangus	syndactylus	Siamangs	Endangered
Nomascus	anamensis	Northern buffed-cheeked gibbon	Critical
	concolor	Concolor or black-crested	Endangered
	nasutus	Eastern black-crested	Critical
	hainanus	Hainan	Critical
	leucogenys	Northern white-cheeked	Critical
	siki	Southern white-cheeked	Endangered
	gabriellae	Yellow-cheeked or golden-cheeked	Endangered

I believe that if more people knew about gibbons and their situation, then more people would be likely to act to prevent the extinction of these fascinating and beautiful small apes. This book is written in an attempt to do a small "something" to encourage this process. For you, the reader, your mission is clear. Inform others about gibbons! A lot is at stake. The songs in the forests need to continue to be heard. The forest canopy must ring with gibbon singing. Silence can be loud when you are used to a wonderful sound.

Why Are Gibbons Endangered?

Why are gibbons endangered? When I asked grade six students what they wanted to know about gibbons, a good number said they wanted to find out about gibbon predators. It was the second most-asked question. This makes sense. Predators that are too successful can endanger species that are prey, such as gibbons.

My quick, filled-with-attitude answer to the students' question was: "We are the main predators of gibbons." Then I pointed out the ways in which humans pose a threat to gibbons. There are other predators too, of course. But compared to us, they have relatively little effect on the gibbon population. What the other predators do would not be enough to cause gibbon numbers to fall as drastically as they have.

These small-time predators include the local big cats. There are a great many of these, all but one of which I had never heard of before doing research on the subject. These predators had been as invisible to me as was their prey to most people in the West. They include clouded leopards (*Neofelis nebulosa*), leopard cats (*Prionailurus bengalensis*), leopards (*Panthera pardus*), Asiatic tigers (*Panthera tigris*), marbled cats (*Pardofelis marmorata*), and Asian golden cats (*Pardofelis temminckii*). Fortunately, the gibbons can move faster than the cats, and sleep much higher than those cats can normally reach. Lower down and on the ground (where gibbons have traditionally been seldom found), the big cats have a distinct advantage. There is good news for gibbons that is bad news for the big cats who are predators of gibbons. These cats are not very likely to pose a greater threat to gibbons in the future, as all of them are threatened (or may soon be threatened) themselves. Their numbers are diminishing in gibbon territory. And it is not because they are running out of gibbons to eat. We, the master predators, with whole forests as our prey, are driving both predators and prey to extinction.

Large snakes are another type of gibbon predator. Here we are looking at various species of python (*Python curtus, brongersmai, breitensteini, molurus, reticulatus* and *timoriensis*), all of which are relatively large snakes. They can pose a threat, but they certainly are not fast over any significant distance. And they cannot reach the canopy or the tops of the big trees, where the gibbons sleep and when the little apes are most potentially vulnerable. Like the large cats, large snakes are small-time players when it comes to endangering gibbons.

Owls and eagles, such as black eagles (*Ictinaetus malayensis*), crested serpent eagles (*Silornis cheela*), mountain hawk eagles (*Spizaetus nipalensis*), and changeable hawk eagles (*Spizaetus cirrhatus*), may occasionally be predators of gibbons while the apes are high in the trees. Black eagles, for example, cruise very slowly just slightly above the forest canopy, and so are effective predators of the small mammals and birds that live there. But as with the other non-human predators, their effects on the gibbon population have been minimal.

Today, with the forests in which gibbons live being cut down, and with gibbons having to more often travel on the ground to find good food and trees to sleep in, it may well be that the leading non-human predator will soon become large domestic dogs. They are faster than gibbons when on the ground; after all, quadrupeds are generally faster than bipeds (unless the latter are kangaroos, and the former are porcupines).

Gibbons' primary defense mechanisms against these animal predators are speed, sound, and the height of sleeping locations (with mothers with infants sleeping in the highest spots). No one moves as fast in the trees as gibbons do. Their wonderful singing voices can also be used to warn others of the presence of predators. There are even sounds and songs specific to certain predators. And those voices can travel a long way. The siamang warning system is especially efficient, as they are the loudest of the gibbons. None of this, however, effectively protects gibbons against human predation. Hiding from us doesn't help much either. We just chop down the hiding places.

Dangers to Gibbon Survival Caused by Humans

DEFORESTATION

There are several major things that humans do which threaten gibbon survival. But there is a warning I want to issue first. It is easy but wrong to simply condemn the local people of Southeastern Asia for the loss of gibbons. Remember how many species that people in the West (think North America and Europe) have driven to extinction or near-extinction by their economic, cultural and agricultural practices. All human populations are to blame for extinction of species. No one population is blameless. No one group is entirely to blame.

In Southeastern Asia, in countries such as Thailand, Malaysia and Indonesia, western-driven globalization results in much of the deforestation that takes place. Check the products on your kitchen shelves for palm oil as an ingredient. The margarine that I used for breakfast a few

John Steckley

minutes ago contained palm oil. I did not know that before I checked. I guess I will be changing brands, if I can find one that does not contain palm oil. Many of the forests that provide habitat for gibbons have been cut down to enable oil-palm farming. Because orangutans live in these same forests, organizations trying to save orangutans are encouraging consumers to switch to alternatives to palm oil. These organizations know me, as I often express to them my wish that they use gibbons as well as orangutans as poster children for endangerment due to deforestation.

Deforestation is the number one threat to every species of gibbon. Trees are cut down, forest fires are deliberately lit, all in the name of acquiring timber and charcoal (for heating and cooking), as well as clearing land for the cultivation of a number of different trees and bushes that can be harvested (e.g., oil palms, pines, rubber trees, and the tea plant [*Camellia sinensis*]). Forests are also cut down in order to produce wide-open grazing spaces for cattle and other livestock. Poor families destroy forest habitat to collect firewood (again for heat and cooking). These practices are difficult to change, especially for the poor. They don't have a lot of choice.

However, over the last few decades a number of national parks and sanctuaries have been created. Still, even there, habitat destruction is a factor, with the illegal but widely practiced cutting down and selling of trees. Enforcement is difficult in the jungle.

Take the Indonesian island of Java, home of the silvery or Javan gibbon, as a dramatic example of deforestation. Based on official governmental statistics (and they are probably an underestimate), the deforestation rate from 2003 to 2006 was 2,500 hectares annually, for a total of 10,000 hectares. That's a bit more than 24,710 acres or about 38.6 square miles (or 16,666 CFL football fields). Forestry officials have calculated that by 2010, there were only about 10,000 hectares of forest still left on the island. That does not leave much room for the silvery gibbons. They will be doing a lot more travelling on the ground between trees in the future.

All is not bad news, however, concerning deforestation. Continual deforestation is not inevitable. For example, in Thailand, where flooding due to deforestation has been officially recognized as being a serious problem, agroforestry (sometimes called forest gardening or forest farming) has been introduced. This involves crops being planted in fields that also contain a significant number of trees. If this can occur in areas where the trees are very tall, very gibbon-worthy, this could potentially save a great deal of gibbon habitat, and therefore, a great number of gibbons.

On the island of Siberut (former home of Toga, the Kloss's gibbon discussed in the previous chapter), although there is still logging going on, and although the 65% of land still forested in 1982 has now fallen to the point that only 52% of the land is still forested, the Siberut Conservation Programme holds out hope for both gibbons and the forest. Under the initiative, biological research is carried out at a 4,500-hectare research station, with scholars coming from around the world. Key to its future success is community-based conservation. This means working with local people to encourage the use of solar energy instead of burning wood, helping to create marketing opportunities for agroforestry products and beginning the development of ecotourism. Among the staff are German and Indonesian administrators, an all-Indonesian field team, and researchers and volunteers from all over the world. You yourself might want to get involved someday, possibly first as a volunteer, and maybe later as a researcher. You would be helping the gibbons, as well as learning a lot.

GIBBON TOURISM

One of the "exotic" experiences offered to westerners travelling in South-eastern Asia has long been what I am calling "gibbon tourism." This is not ecotourism, where jungle tours could involve gibbon spotting, with (hopefully) little destructive impact on the gibbons involved. Instead, it entails (among other things) foreign tourists having their pictures taken alongside gibbons on leashes in places such as the large city of Bangkok, or on the beaches and at the bars and restaurants of Phuket, a popular tourist destination island. Both Bangkok and Phuket are in Thailand, where several species of gibbon live.

These gibbon "photo ops" take place on the streets, in marketplaces or in bars. Tourists view them as a unique opportunity for an experience that can be shared on Facebook with friends and family back home. A gibbon photo opportunity doesn't cost much, generally between six and seven American dollars. Such tourists fail to think about the consequences of the trade that they are supporting. The photo models are badly treated. For instance, to appear photogenic or cute, gibbons are sometimes forced to smoke cigarettes, drink alcohol, eat candy or wear baby clothes. None of this is good for the gibbon. Nor are the drugs that are sometimes forced upon the ordinarily active gibbons to keep them quiet. A normal, healthy adult gibbon might bite a human who came too close—not good for picture-taking profits. The lives of the gibbons having their pictures taken is often neither long nor happy. Young gibbons are generally friendlier and less dangerous than their elders. Older gibbons have bigger teeth and are more likely to use them on tourists.

In the following section, we consider one small example—about 12 pounds—of the consequences of gibbon tourist photography, but with a conclusion that was good for the gibbon involved.

MIMI'S STORY

At the Highland Farm and Gibbon Sanctuary, in a 35-acre reforested area near the Thailand-Burma border, there lives a female gibbon named Mimi. Before she was rescued and brought to this place, she worked as a tourist photo-opportunity gibbon in Bangkok. One day, during her brutal bondage in Bangkok (I like the way that combination of words sounds), Mimi tried to escape by climbing up a pole. Unfortunately for her, it was an electrical pole and she grasped a live cable with predictably disastrous results. She received a large electrical charge (and not one like the bill we receive every month). As a result, her left forearm and lower left leg had to be amputated, and she was blinded in one eye. Her owner discarded her as useless in the photo tourism trade. A gibbon with a partial arm and leg would not be considered cute. Fortunately, the people of the Highland Farm and Gibbon Sanctuary found out about her situation and brought her to the sanctuary. She had become, after a bad start, one very, very lucky gibbon.

The Highland Farm and Gibbon Sanctuary was founded by American William E. Deters and his Thai wife Pharanee. The couple met and married in the United States, but decided to retire on a farm in Thailand in 1991. A local hunter had shot a mother gibbon, and was left with an infant daughter. He took her to the Deters, hoping to sell the gibbon to them what would amount to between $12 and $14 U.S. In their 24-year marriage, they had never before had a pet, but they couldn't resist the little girl gibbon. She was the only gibbon they had to buy; the rest have all been given to them. They called her Chester, not knowing that she was a girl. (Remember that it is often hard for humans to tell the sex of a gibbon, particularly of an infant. But the gibbons know.) They later had to call her *Miss* Chester. By 1995, they decided to open a sanctuary, now home to more than 40 gibbons of three different species.

It should be pointed out that using primates as tourist-photography models is not a practice confined to southeastern Asia. Apes and monkeys have been rescued from beach photographers in Europe (particularly Spain, where the practice is now illegal), the Middle East, Africa and the Americas. Their cuteness and exotic nature sometimes act against the best interests of the little guys.

Laws against Trade in Exotic Pets

In 1975, all species of gibbons were included in the provisions of the Convention on International Trade in Endangered Species of Fauna and Flora (known as CITES). This agreement made illegal the international trade in species designated as endangered. Different countries signed on to this agreement at different times. Indonesia did so in 1979, for example. The agreement now applies wherever gibbons live in the wild. To the best of my knowledge, the market in gibbons as pets is illegal everywhere. But it still takes place despite the laws enacted.

The following Indonesian law shows what an anti-pet and anti-trade law looks like. The law makes it illegal to:

> Catch, injure, care for, transport, and trade in a protected animal [such as a gibbon] in a live condition;
>
> Keep, possess, care for, transport, and trade in a protected animal in a dead condition;
>
> Transfer a protected animal from one place to another, within or outside Indonesia;
>
> Trade, keep or possess skin, bodies, or other parts of a protected animal or the goods made of parts of the animal, or transfer from one place in Indonesia to another, within or outside Indonesia.

Penalties that can be imposed when these laws are broken can add up, including fines of up to about $9,600 U.S., and up to five years imprisonment. One of the problems, however, is that prosecution requires considerable police resources, which are relatively hard to come by. Despite the opposition of police forces around the world, the illegal international trade in exotic pets still flourishes to varying degrees in different lands. There are several reasons why. Often people report simply not knowing about the laws forbidding the practice. In some cases, I accept that as a legitimate reason. Every country, province, state, county, city and town has a spaghetti-ball of complicated laws that everyone cannot be expected to know. A few years ago, one of my dogs bit someone. Although I know that it is against the law to kill, to steal, to run naked down Main Street and to park a car overnight on my street, I did *not* know what the law expected of a dog owner in such a situation. Neither did anyone I spoke with, including several people who had dogs. While ignorance of the law is said to be no excuse, it certainly can be common (particularly when it comes to small town bylaws).

The ability of central governments to communicate effectively to people living in the countryside in those regions where gibbons are still found in the wild is not generally as efficient as such communication in the West (and sometimes *that* isn't very efficient, as we all know). So in the past sometimes people could legitimately say that they did not know that owning gibbons was illegal. In Thailand, it wasn't until 1992 that a law made gibbon ownership illegal. However, government and gibbon rescue agencies are improving local people's awareness of such laws, so ignorance is less widespread and less of an excuse.

Unfortunately, the black-market pet trade in gibbons is still profitable. Do not be fooled by what look like low prices for gibbons. In 2009, it was reported that in Indonesia gibbons were selling for between U.S. $10 and $100 each. This is a significant amount of money for poor people struggling to survive.

It should be pointed out that the illegal trade does not just encompass gibbons as pets. The biomedical industry (including drug and medical research companies) includes some of the most powerful and profitable corporations on the planet. They have spent substantial sums on the purchase of gibbons. Remember that we share about 95% of our genetic makeup with gibbons. This close connection makes them prime candidates for medical and cosmetic research. This is especially true because gibbons are much less visible to the general public than their better-known and popular cousins, the orangutans, gorillas, chimpanzees, and bonobos. People in the West have become aware of much that happens to *them* in labs. I have signed many a petition opposing medical research on monkeys and chimpanzees, but I have never seen such a petition concerning gibbons. In this sense, too, remaining invisible is dangerous for the small apes.

Finally, while zoos near you no doubt act within the law when they acquire gibbons, that cannot be said for all zoos everywhere.

Death in the Pet Trade

In his study of white-handed gibbons in Thailand, C. R. Carpenter wrote, "The traveler in the Far East will often find gibbons being kept as household pets." At every stage of the illegal trade in pet gibbons, the little apes die. The generally preferred method of obtaining infant gibbons for the trade involves shooting and killing the mother. For every infant gibbon adopted as a pet, it is said that at least five other gibbons die. With the intimate and intense emotional ties as well as very close physical connection that gibbon infants and their mothers share, sometimes the little ones fail to survive as orphans. Those who do survive are transported to market in carrying cases or cages that are too small. The horrible food and living conditions and severe stress of life in the marketplace also take their toll.

Even when they become pets, they often do not live long. Bad feeding practices appear to be common. No pet food companies produce nutritious gibbon food ("Figs for Physical Fitness"). It is unlikely that helpful traditional knowledge about what to feed your gibbon exists, because historically gibbons were rarely kept as pets in countries where they are found in the wild.

When Wild Pets Grow Up

When I was 11 years old, I wanted to have a pet raccoon. I had fed them by hand when they came to the door of a friend's cottage. I was disappointed when I was told, quite rightly, that as cute and nice as they are as babies, they get nasty when they get older. What that means is that as adults they have both the weapons (teeth and claws) and strength to inflict wounds and pain on the people that keep them, when they feel their independence is being restricted. I learned as a child that baby wild things are fun, but they are dangerous when they grow up. That same friend of mine had a baby snapping turtle, too. I wanted one, but was told that I could not have one.

My wife Angie and I have a weakness for baby parrots. That is why we have eight parrots now, one a young cockatiel named Gus who is on my shoulder as I type these words. We have been to sanctuaries where abandoned parrots live. They are usually the big ones, the macaws (they're the biggest), the Amazons, and the cockatoos. The big birds can be problematic as adolescents (they become teenagers young and stay that way for a long time). Our yellow-headed Amazon, Lime, is like that. She is sometimes (my wife Angie would say often) a bird brat. And Amazons are armed with big weapons with their sharp hooked beaks. I think that is one major reason why you pretty much only see the big guys in the sanctuaries. They became too much bird for their owners. Lime alone is a lot of bird (but we love her).

The same can be said of gibbons. They are very cute as infants. If Penelope had needed a home, if we had the money to set up a gibbon sanctuary in our backyard, if we could have obtained a license to own her, and if it were not against the law in our town, province and country, we would have taken her immediately. That's a lot of ifs. But when gibbons mature they have mature gibbon teeth. In one visit with Penelope, she touched her teeth to my hand in play. No harm was intended, and no pain resulted. Now that she's an adult, I would have to be a lot more careful around her and her big teeth. Her keeper made a point of telling me that before I visited her this year: wise words.

Carpenter wrote about what happens to pet gibbons who become adults:

> The fate of these captive gibbons is determined by their growing old and relatively inactive or perhaps increasingly vicious. When they cease to be entertaining and become dangerous they are released, sold or even killed.

In reading both *Gibbons in the Family* and *Are You Ready for Love, Tomoko?*, I found that the authors talked about reaching the dangerous-to-be-with stage with their beloved gibbon pets. They had to give them up, either to a zoo or a sanctuary, as their pets had become a danger to family members, servants and friends. It wasn't easy, but it was necessary.

Unfortunately, many—perhaps most—people who live in gibbon countries do not have the funds or the social connections that these authors had and that allowed them to give up their pet gibbons to institutions where the small primates will be well-cared-for. The alternative is to abandon them in the woods, where captive-raised gibbons with no rehabilitation enabling them to take care of themselves are not well-equipped to survive. The illegal pet trade in gibbons needs to be stopped so that no gibbon is put into such a terrible situation again.

Hunting Gibbons

TABOOS

My reading suggests to me that in many places where gibbons live, people did not traditionally hunt them. In some areas, at least, this was because there was a taboo against hunting and eating gibbons. *Taboos* (a word coming from the Tongan language, which is related to the languages of Indonesia and Malaysia) are prohibitions against particular acts which are considered dangerous and disgusting, not merely illegal. In the West we have a taboo against eating dogs. The white-with-black-spots creature at my feet as I write is happy about that taboo, as is the appetizingly named wiener dog a little farther away.

The Tangsa of northeastern India have long had a taboo against hunting gibbons. Even seeing a gibbon on a hunting trip was said to bring bad fortune. What's more, just saying the word for gibbon, *lungkhang*, was taboo. You had to be really angry to say that word, as you might be if you were trying (unsuccessfully) to program your television so that you could watch a show on Australian parrots, or if you had just been bitten in the toe by a Senegal parrot (both things that have really happened to me).

There is a traditional Tangsa story about the origin of this taboo. In this story, a beautiful young woman named Youngmo went out into the rice fields alone, where she met and fell in love with a young hoolock male. (Youngmo must have been a good climber.) When she came back day after day with her clothing in a mess, her family got suspicious. Her brother went out to the field and killed his sister's hairy boyfriend. When Youngmo returned to the rice field, she saw the hoolock's bloody skin hanging from the wall of a hut next to the field. I'll bet she said "lungkhang" that day, particularly when talking with and about her brother.

Another people of northeastern India, the Maran, were and possibly still are a clan-based society. Clans are divisions of societies that are based on the idea that all members of a clan are related. Often the story of the origin of the clan talks about the common ancestor of the people. Among the Maran, there was a clan named Houlouokhown, translated as "Hoolock or gibbon eaten," referring to their not being permitted to eat gibbons. It is often true among clan-based societies that you do not eat the animal that gives the clan its name. I was adopted as an adult into the Turtle clan of the Wyandot. Fortunately, when I was 11 years old and dreaming of being a biologist, I watched a female painted turtle dig a hole and lay eggs in it. That day I vowed never to eat turtle. I was a very serious 11-year-old and biologist-wannabe. I have kept that personal taboo for over 50 years.

In one version of the origin story of the Gibbon Eaten clan of the Maran, two brothers cut down all the trees in an area except for two or three. Then, they set a massive fire to burn the remaining plants and brush piles. A hoolock gibbon was in one of the remaining trees. His eyes blinded by smoke, he leapt from his tree to escape, not knowing that there were no other trees to leap to. He literally crashed and burned. The brothers come back after a few days. Seeing the cooked meat of the gibbon, they assumed that it was a deer and they ate it. When they find out what it was that they had eaten, the taboo against eating gibbon meat was put in place.

Taboos also reflected traditional beliefs and environmental relationships. Globalization has changed matters. I believe that a significant increase in gibbon hunting resulted from greater contact between tribal people and people from the outside world, who violated all kinds of taboos and rules of life and survived unpunished.

Tony Whitten reported how local taboos against hunting Kloss's gibbons on Siberut were called "sinful" by one misguided missionary. He did not consider that orthodox Jews and Muslims don't eat pork and conservative Hindus don't eat beef, all part of their dedication to their religious beliefs. And what about not eating meat on Fridays, a traditional practice for Catholics? Isn't that a food taboo? The missionary therefore foolishly and harmfully encouraged people to hunt gibbons, even though that was illegal.

But it has been the economics of globalization that seems to have become the biggest reason for hunting gibbons.

GLOBALIZATION AND GIBBONS

Urban people in the West tend to provide themselves with food, housing, clothing and the other necessities by having one job. In rural communities—in the West but especially in Asian countries—it's often necessary to combine several activities to earn a living. And these activities may require people to act as resource entrepreneurs or opportunists, adding new plant and animal species to those they traditionally relied on. I think of the example of the Newfoundland fishery (I lived in Newfoundland for several years as a graduate student and professor). When the cod-fishing moratorium was imposed, snow crab and northern shrimp that had been traditionally eaten by cod and the area's other diminished fish populations became a new resource for Newfoundland fishermen to exploit.

There are markets for gibbon bodies that have encouraged people to hunt gibbons in greater numbers. One market is for medicine. For example, in the Chinese market, there is growing demand for ground-up gibbon bones. Why is that? One explanation is this. Rheumatism is a crippling disorder that affects many people in China and around the world. It severely limits the mobility of individuals afflicted by it. They walk and generally move in a very stiff manner. Gibbons are widely known in China and neighbouring countries to move freely and fast with great flexibility. And they don't seem to get rheumatism. Therefore the idea arose that using gibbon bones as medicine would make people more like gibbons, flexible and faster moving. This is the same principle motivating people in the West to use shark cartilage to prevent cancer. Sharks do not get cancer for complicated reasons relating to their being an early or "primitive" kind of fish. It has nothing to do with their cartilage. But the principle is still compelling if you don't think too deeply or scientifically.

Recognizing that people are hunting gibbons because of financial need is a big step toward stopping the practice. To end this otherwise rather depressing chapter on a positive note, we will look briefly at an institution that is working to save the gibbons. Its story also makes a nice transition into the next chapter.

WORKING TO SAVE GIBBONS

The Khao Yai Conservation Project (KYCP), in Thailand, was initiated in 2000 with the goal of reducing the illegal poaching or hunting of gibbons and other endangered species. Several players were involved in this hopeful project. On the governmental level, the Thai Royal Forest Department and the U.S. State Department partnered in the project. Non-governmental agencies also participated, including the Wildlife Conservation Society (WCS) and Wild Aid (now known as Wildlife Alliance). The KYCP followed a two-pronged approach, working both on the ranger and the poacher side. I believe that is the only kind of strategy that can work effectively.

For two years I worked for the Wildlife Branch of the Ontario Ministry of Natural Resources. Speaking with conservation officers in my home province, I learned how it was often difficult to enforce laws dedicated to the conservation of various mammal and bird species because of the large distances and dense forests involved. And this was with the benefit of modern technology (but before cell phones). Imagine how much more difficult it would be to work as a conservation officer or ranger in Thailand, where there are dense jungles, and where rangers have less access to modern equipment. With the KYCP, the rangers were given technology and training that improved their ability to both find and catch gibbon poachers.

Just as important was finding alternative sources of income for people working in and around the gibbon forests. Change the economics of their lives, and you lower the frequency of gibbon poaching. Figures vary. It is very difficult to accurately determine poaching rates, because those engaged in it try very hard not to be seen or caught (and therefore counted). However, it seems that everyone agrees that there is less poaching going on now than before the creation of the KYCP. Much needs to be done, but this is a good start in the right direction.

Conclusion

Don't let this chapter get you down! Yes, all 17 species of gibbon are endangered, but actions are being taken to help save the gibbons. As you will see in the next chapter, there are people around the world actively helping the gibbons, both in their native lands, and in countries where gibbons live only in sanctuaries and zoos. You can help them too, no matter where you live.

CHAPTER SEVEN
Gibbon Rescue

T
he last chapter was mostly doom and gloom concerning the possible near-future fate of the gibbons. I now will present some good news, some cause for optimism so as to end the book on a happy note. Fortunately, there is good reason to be positive about gibbons' future. A growing number of people (professional scientists, citizen scientists and non-scientist volunteers) and institutions are doing useful work to rescue gibbons of many species from extinction. Unfortunately, too few people know much about these wonderful gibbon rescue workers and the important work that they are doing. Like the animals they love and are helping to survive, these good people are largely invisible, too. We will try in this chapter to reduce their invisibility with some positive stories. There are more out there.

Human Heroes of the Gibbons

WHAT ONE WOMAN CAN DO: DR. SHIRLEY MCGREAL

Remember the stories about Igor and Arun Rangsi from Chapter 5? Do you recall how they were rescued? They were laboratory gibbons, saved from pain, sickness and early death by the International Primate Protection League (IPPL). Now you can learn a little bit about the woman most responsible for saving them, the founder of the IPPL, Dr. Shirley McGreal.

Dr. Shirley McGreal is a native of Cheshire, in northwestern England. During the years 1969–71, when she was engaged in the research work in India that would earn her a Ph.D. (and the right to put "Doctor" in front of her name), she became aware of gibbons and the dangers threatening their survival. She moved to Thailand, where she was emotionally touched by seeing gibbons in tiny crates offered up for sale in the marketplace and then trapped in confining cages in their owner's yards.

These experiences changed her life. She felt that the gibbons deserved better than that. But first she needed to learn more about these small apes. To do so, McGreal contacted experts on the larger apes. She spoke with Jane Goodall, famous for her work with chimpanzees, and was also was able to contact Dian Fossey, whose life and work were profiled in the book and movie *Gorillas in the Mist*. McGreal also communicated with Birute Galdikas, who has long studied and laboured to save from extinction Indonesia's orangutans. Inspired by what these famous primatologist women (nicknamed the "Trimates" because there are three of them) were doing, and eager to dedicate her life, as they had, to understanding and rescuing apes, Dr. McGreal founded the International Primate Protection League (IPPL) in 1973. From a very small beginning, the IPPL has grown to the point it has more than 15,000 members and supporters (that could include you). Realizing that she would need a location that provided sanctuary for gibbons and other animals in danger, McGreal in 1977 established just such a safe haven in the South Carolina countryside.

McGreal's first gibbon success story was that of Arun Rangsi, who, as we read in Chapter 5, made the IPPL sanctuary his home in 1981. He still lives there, too. Now the ten-acre sanctuary is home to some 34 (or so) gibbons, as well as some rescued otters and a few dogs.

The word "activist" tends to be overused to the point of losing its meaning. Dr. Shirley McGreal is a genuine ACTIVIST. She does not just save individual gibbons, although, as we have seen, that work is important. She has a long history of identifying particular practices that are dangerous and painful to gibbons, and working to end those practices through aggressive, sometimes dangerous action on her part. One such story that very much impressed me is the undercover work she did while researching an important and revealing article, "The Singapore Connection," that took aim at animal smuggling in Southeast Asia.

Here is what happened. McGreal went undercover and became a spy for gibbons. She played the role of someone who wanted to import gibbons and other animals by ship from Southeast Asia to the United States. The trick worked. She was given a great deal of information from people who were masters of that illegal trade. She obtained a price list that included:

Gibbon Species	Price (U.S. $)
Agile	$150
White-handed	$150
Hoolock	$150
Blackcap	$180
Siamang	$200

With the publication of her articles in 1975 and 1976, the smugglers and their practices were exposed. It is thought by some (and I am one of them) that her work was one of the most significant factors that led to making trading in gibbons illegal in Thailand, which is near Singapore. Some people walk their talk. In this case, she ran with her plan.

Another practice that Dr. McGreal early opposed and exposed was the use of gibbons as unwilling subjects in medical and in psychological research. In the IPPL newsletter of March, 1976, she focused on one such research activity: the Hall's Island Gibbon Project. Here is what she revealed to the world (or at least her readers) in the article.

In June 1970, there was established on Hall's Island, part of the small Atlantic country of Bermuda, a "free-ranging" gibbon colony of nine. The gibbons had been illegally imported from Thailand five years after that country had banned the capture, trade and export of gibbons. Hall's Island was a research colony. The name of the medical/psychological research project being carried out was "Experimental Modification of Behavior in an Open-Field Situation Using Gibbons." The experiments involved dosing the defenseless little apes with heavy-duty drugs and carrying out metal brain implants. The researchers were trying to see whether by using these powerful and destructive means they could influence the thinking and behaviour of gibbons. This wasn't because they wanted to use gibbons as mindless slaves or furry soldiers (say for a remake of *Planet of the Apes*), although I wonder if that idea didn't occur to some of the more danger-ously imaginative researchers. The underlying reason for the experiment was the Cold War, the struggle between countries in the West (primarily North America and Western Europe) and those countries that were part of or controlled by the USSR (the Union of Soviet Socialist Republics), which was dominated by Russia and later collapsed in 1991. It was a time of spies vs. spies. Watch an old James Bond movie and you can understand something of what the thinking was like. Anything the Russians did was closely monitored. Misleading rumour could easily become thought of as fact.

Some politicians in the West had heard that the Soviets had developed means of brainwashing people, controlling their thoughts and their actions. Several popular movies reflected that theme. What they had heard was not true. There was no such methodology then and is none now. But because some Western scientists feared the enemy had made this break-through, they believed that they needed to do similar research of their own, possibly learning how to do their own brainwashing. They did not want to fall behind in the Cold War (so called because it was not "hot" with large-scale battles and shooting, but more a matter of spying, trickery and smaller-scale—though still destructive—wars such as the ones in Vietnam and Korea). Many research subjects, both human (for example, psychiatric patients and prisoners) and animal (particularly primates because they are our closest relatives), suffered needlessly because of ill-conceived and un-necessary research.

In the IPPL newsletter, Dr. McGreal reported how within two years, six of the nine founding members of the gibbon colony on Hall's Island had died. The scientists seemed puzzled by the death of their research subjects but at the same time they did not appear to question the ethics or morality of their practices, and the clear role these played in killing the gibbons. McGreal believed that public opinion could help shut the project down. Bermuda's laws included a requirement to exercise "reasonable care and supervision" when working with animals. McGreal's work was important in providing an alternative and informed voice that called into question scientists' attitudes towards gibbons as research subjects, in this study and in others. Science requires continual dialogue among different voices and viewpoints to advance and be respected. Questioning the ethical assump-tions underlying research, as McGreal so powerfully did and does, must be part of that dialogue. Scientists often ask the question "How do we do this?" but can be a little neglectful concerning the equally important ques-tion of "*Should* we do this?"

Dr. McGreal has been justly rewarded for her work by Queen Elizabeth II. In 2008, she received an OBE, the prestigious Order of the British Empire. I am sure that the gibbons have rewarded her as well, in their long-armed hairy ways, with recognition hugs (a gibbon OBE—**O**ne **B**ig **E**mbrace) and much more.

WHAT ONE MAN CAN DO: ALAN MOOTNICK

The defining moment of Alan Mootnick's life—what television sports-casters would call the turning point—occurred when he was nine years old. This was when he heard, for the first time, the songs of the gibbons, at the Los Angeles Zoo near his California home. "When I closed my eyes and listened to their voices it made me feel as if I was in the forest," he later remembered. No matter what else happened in his life—the death of his parents while he was still young, or his early career as a combination car mechanic, welder and house painter—those sounds in his mind could not be silenced. He must have felt that they were calling him to join with them in some way. I know from Carmen and Samson how those songs can affect a person.

If there can be two turning points, two defining moments in a life (and there can), the second one came when Mootnick was 25, in 1976. Someone gave him his first gibbon, a young male named "Spanky." The owner could (or would) no longer take care of the little fellow. Spanky was Alan's first rescue gibbon. It would not by a long shot be his last.

From that beginning Mootnick set up the Gibbon Conservation Center (GCC) in Santa Clarita, California. He had little money of his own to do so, and had to sell most of his possessions to get the project started. It was initially difficult for him to ask for donations. It probably felt like begging to him. He couldn't support a large staff to begin with, and never would have one. The GCC is small, only five acres, with a tiny staff of three, but many volunteers help in this very important work. Mootnick even answered the phone himself (as you will see shortly).

Mootnick became one of the leading experts on gibbons, writing articles for scientific journals, but did so as a self-taught expert. He did not study biology at university. As a college professor, I should not be recommending that students reading this book take this path to knowledge. Being self-taught in a science such as biology is a long and difficult path, often resulting in gaping holes in a person's knowledge. There are few people as driven and as talented as Alan Mootnick. Pursue the academic route if you can. But then I catch myself. I myself have never learned about gibbons in a classroom, just from books, articles and direct contact. Writers and the gibbons themselves have taught me most of what I know about the little guys. They are my teachers; their books, articles and compounds, my classrooms.

Mootnick's sanctuary has been a definite success. As many as 44 gibbons who have been rescued have lived there at one time—the most gibbons living in any sanctuary or zoo in the Americas. The ropes and branches in that place must be constantly moving!

In particular, the GCC has specialized in working to help the rare and endangered pileated gibbon, or *Hylobates pileatus*. It has the only successful breeding program in the western hemisphere for that species.

Of course, the GCC also has white-handed gibbons there. The blond mother of Penelope, one of the stars of Chapter 4, grew up there. When I called the GCC in 2010, Alan answered the phone and was able to find information about her for me. I began to appreciate him from that point onward. He didn't fob off the job on someone else.

One other benefit offered by the GCC needs to be stated: *awareness*. Over the years, thousands of school children have gone there and become aware of gibbons, and of their threatened status. Gibbons certainly are visible in California because of Alan Mootnick's work.

Unfortunately, Alan Mootnick died on November 4, 2011, at only 60 years of age. One small but beautiful tribute to his life is that a gibbon infant born that Christmas was named "Alan Mootnick." The people at the GCC call him "Little Alan." As long-armed in body as Alan Mootnick was in soul, the little gibbon will, like Big Alan, reach out to touch a lot of people.

AURÉLIEN BRULÉ AND THE KALAWEIT GIBBON PROTECTION PROGRAM

While the IPPL was developed by an English woman working in the United States, and the GCC was developed in the same country by an American man, the Kalaweit Gibbon Protection Program began with a French man working on the Pacific island of Borneo, a long way from home.

As with Thomas Mootnick, this Frenchman's love for gibbons began while young when he visited a zoo. At age 12, Aurélien Brulé fell in love with gibbons. When he was 13, he was hired by a local zoo. He spent hours every day observing and listening to them (as well as doing his work, I might add). Once, when he was depressed, a white-handed gibbon reached out to him and held his hand. As you know, I can understand the power and beauty of such hand-to-hand contact. *Hylobates lar* became special to him, a favourite of his. By the time he was 17, he had published a work entitled "Le Gibbon à mains blanche" ("White-handed Gibbons"). When he was 18, he moved to Thailand. People there, when they saw his love for gibbons, would call him "Chanee," which means *gibbon* in the Thai language. In 1998, at 19, he set up and became program director and president of the Kalaweit Gibbon Protection Program (KGPP).

The KGPP began its active work in 1999. Its main office is in Bukit Baka Bukit Raya National Park in Kalimantan, the Indonesian section of the island of Borneo. The organization has four sites, three on Borneo, and one on the nearby island of Sumatra. Its activities are directed as helping six species of gibbon: *Hylobates muelleri, H. albibarbis, H. agilis, H. lar, H. klossii* and siamangs *(Symphalangus syndactylus)*. The program has three main elements: gibbon rehabilitation, habitat protection and education.

When rescued gibbons arrive, they are put into quarantine at the Kalaweit Care Centre. The word *kalaweit*, by the way, means "gibbon" in the local Dayak Ngaju language. When the gibbons are ready to leave their compound, they are released onto large pieces of land controlled by the KGPP. In 2007, two families of *H. albibarbis* (white-bearded—like me—gibbons), each with a mother, father and child, were released into Hampapak Reserve. So far, it seems that the family has survived in the woods, a success story. Two pairs of the same species were set free on Mintin Island, and a pair of siamangs were let go to roam wild on Kalaweit Sumatra. The numbers may seem small, but the true success lies in developing a working procedure for others to follow. We won't say these gibbons are first on a path that many others will walk, because as pretty much full-time tree-dwellers, gibbons don't follow paths. Maybe we can say "tree trails" instead. And as brachiators gibbons swing much more than they walk. Let's just say these gibbons are first on the branch on the fig tree of freedom.

Key to the overall success of the KGPP is working with the local people, teaching them ways of increasing the chances for gibbons to survive, while not taking away from their own economic survival. KGPP has done this well, acting with respect for the culture of the local people, and for the people themselves. The lessons are simple: Do not keep gibbons as pets. When gibbons are kept as pets, there are health risks for both gibbons and humans. Do not hunt and kill gibbons. Do not buy or sell gibbons. Part of the respect for the culture is realizing that the practices the KGPP is introducing can mean less money and food for people, so the organization is working to provide alternative jobs, as well as funding for schools and medical care. Giving to the gibbons means helping local people, so that they are not forced into desperate, gibbon-threatening measures.

One effective method has been inviting local children stay overnight at the sanctuary to get to know the gibbons currently residing there. The knowledge the children gain from direct experience reinforces the simple messages of the program. And the kids take ownership of the fight for gibbon survival.

Another method involves radio, beginning with the KGPP buying time on local radio stations, and then setting up Kalaweit FM:

> This radio station is aimed at [a] young audience and broadcasts popular music, current affairs programs, and comedy shows. Five times per hour, conservation messages are broadcast on a variety of topics including bat hunting, forest fires, and [the need to refrain from] the keeping of gibbons and other wild animals as pets.

The message seems to be working, as, according to their website, 20 gibbons have been voluntarily surrendered to the people of KGPP. That wasn't happening before.

But education is not just confined to the local people. The invisibility of gibbons in the West has to be addressed as well. Without help from people all over the world, gibbon rescue is not possible. One way of educating Westerners used by the KGPP is to provide what it calls its eco-volunteer program. The program offers an opportunity for fit people with the financial means to pay for their own travel and living costs and to contribute a little in addition toward the running costs of the program to assist in person with KGPP's work with gibbons, and thus learn from observing gibbon behaviour. If I were a lot younger, and more physically fit, and not the co-keeper of an aviary with eight parrots, I would be there. I hope that there are readers of this book who will at some point in their lives take advantage of this unique opportunity.

Brulé's fight to save the gibbons has not been without danger. He has alerted authorities to illegal logging that takes away precious gibbon habitat. Doing so is obviously not going to be without opposition. In 2009, Brulé and his Indonesian wife Prada were attacked by loggers. Ever since, they have had a guard posted in front of their house.

In March 2013, Brulé published his first book, *Le Sourire Fendu ou l'Histoire de Gibbon* (*The Crooked Smile, or The History of the Gibbon*), with plans to follow up with an English translation. At time of writing, the English version has not been published, but I am looking forward to reading it if it ever is translated. Unfortunately, my French isn't good enough to translate it myself.

Organizations and Projects Involved with Gibbon Rescue
THE SILVERY GIBBON PROJECT AND
THE JAVAN GIBBON RESCUE AND REHABILITATION CENTRE

The Silvery Gibbon Project (SGP) was established in 1991 through the Perth Zoo in western Australia. Its main purpose was the conservation of silvery or Javan gibbons on the island of Java in Indonesia. This kind of conservation is called "*in situ* conservation" (Latin for "in the location"), as opposed to "*ex situ* conservation" ("out of location"), which involves breeding programs in zoos.

I prefer these somewhat clumsy terms to the expressions "in the wild" and "in captivity." It is too easy to think that living in the wild is automatically better and more enjoyable for the gibbons, while living in captivity means unhappy gibbons being locked away in prison cages. A gibbon who lives in an enriched compound with his or her family, taken care of by an enlightened zoo staff, has a lot of freedom, and can get a lot of joy out of life. I've seen it, and you have read about it in an earlier chapter. Living in the wild can be very stressful and restricted by an oppressive human presence. It does not necessarily mean living in freedom.

In 2001, groups concerned about the survival of silvery gibbons got together. These groups included the SGP, Conservation International (through their Indonesian representative, Dr. Jatna Supriatna of the University of Indonesia), the Gungung Gede Pangrano National Park and the Indonesian Ministry of Forestry. Their aim was to plan the establishment of the Javan Gibbon Rescue and Rehabilitation Centre. There was serious concern over the endangered status of the species, especially because of the rapid rate at which Java was becoming deforested. Eventually the fact would emerge that 98 percent of gibbon natural habitat had been destroyed. This earned Java, a heavily populated island of more than 130 million people, the negative "honour" of the 2008 Guinness world record for deforestation. I'm glad it is not an Olympic event. Stories also surfaced that at least 80 Javan gibbons were being kept illegally as pets. As you know, for every incident like this which is reported, many more remain unknown to the authorities. Something had to be done soon.

In 2003, 15 hectares (37 acres) of land in West Java was set aside for the Javan Gibbon Centre (JGC). That's the size of a small farm. The people

who ran the JGC had the short-term goal of taking in donated or confiscated silvery gibbons, and assessing and improving their heath at the
JGC's facilities. That goal might be short-term, but it is still very
important. The longer term goal was to "re-establish viable, free-ranging
populations over the species' historic range." Achieving this goal would
require education of local people, captive-breeding and multi-stage reintroduction into the wild. From the beginning, it was recognized as
important that the permanent staff not be outsiders but, rather, Indo-
nesians, so it wouldn't look as though the program were run by outsiders.
And there had to be long-term commitment to the work. The main ex-
ternal funding agency was the SGP. It, in turn, relies on fund-raising,
including donations from individuals, corporations and other zoos.

By June 2007, the JGC was home to five silvery gibbons: males Kis Kis,
Nakula (see below) and Jeffrey, and females Nancy and Moni. Jeffrey and
Nancy experienced love at first site and quickly became a couple. By the
summer of 2008, there were 28 gibbons, with the main source of new gibbon residents being the Cikananga Rescue Center (CRC). There were now
eight gibbon pairs, including two couples with pregnant females. One pair,
Echi and Septa, who had previously spent almost five years at the CRC,
were chosen as the first to be released into the wild. First they were kept in
an enclosure deep in the woods, so that they would become more accustomed to their new home. Eventually, in October 2009, they were
released.

The education function of the JGC is performed largely through the
Mobile Conservation Education Unit. It uses conservation films and songs,
interactive quizzes and games, as well as a travelling library that is available to local groups. The star of the show is Moli, an animated silvery
gibbon—though I imagine that most silvery gibbons are rather animated!—who is also featured in toys. If you adopt a gibbon by making a
financial contribution to the centre, you become part of "Moli's family."
Gibbons do not usually have big families, but I hope that Moli does. To
find out more about the Javan Gibbon Centre, visit their website at
www.silvery.org.au. It contains good information about gibbons and other
endangered animals, and how you can help them.

One story that personifies (could we possibly say "gibbonifies"?) the
value of the Javan Gibbon Centre is Nakula. Several etymologies of her
name appear on the Internet, making interpretation difficult. The best
explanation in my view is that "Nakula" is a Sanskrit-based female name,

relating to the Hindu goddess Parvati. But Nakula is a male gibbon. Why give him a girl's name? His story might explain that.

He was born sometime in 2001 in Java. When he was still very young, his mother was shot so that he could be taken from her to be made somebody's pet. Evidently kept in unhealthy conditions, out of the sun and in a cage, he developed the bone disorder known as rickets, which stems from a lack of calcium and vitamin D (such as would be provided naturally through the skin's interaction with sunlight). The condition may also have resulted from being fed inappropriate foods (e.g., soft drinks and rice), and being confined indoors. Nakula's legs are deformed and he is missing several toes due to a probable unhealed fracture. When he first arrived at the Cikananga Rescue Center, he was so emaciated, with legs described as looking like "steel pins," that it was thought that he was female. Hence (at least to my way of thinking) he received a girl's name. He was the opposite of Mark, the female Siamang, discussed in Chapter 5.

When the Cikananga Center lost its main sponsor, the IPPL-UK (United Kingdom) assumed responsibility for dealing with the financial fall-out. Funding went to relocating Nakula to the Javan Gibbon Centre early in 2008. When he was x-rayed there, it was seen that there were "quite dramatic curves" in his spine. But there was no new damage, and he was improving in terms of weight, strength, fur and skin condition. In June 2008, in the magazine *Silvery Gibbon Project*, it was declared that the seven-year-old and now mature gibbon "is likely to live out his life at the centre . . . [as he is] . . . not likely to survive in the wild. He is otherwise a healthy animal and with his beautiful nature will make a great ambassador for the species."

With many gibbons entering and passing through the Javan Gibbon Centre, Nakula has developed a good number of gibbon friendships, and is able to be preened.

At the time of writing this book, he was still there, and, according to staff, after years of rejecting close relationships, Nakula now has a girlfriend. Now that's rehabilitation!

MONKEY WORLD APE RESCUE CENTRE

The Monkey World Ape Rescue Centre (MWARC) in Wareham, Dorset, in southern England, was established in 1987. It was the realization of a dream of its founder, New Yorker Jim Cronin. The people at MWARC see their main job as rescuing primates from abuse suffered at the hands of "photographers, the entertainment industry, laboratories, circuses, and the pet trade." Their largest single act of rescue took place in 2008, when they retrieved 88 capuchin monkeys from a medical research laboratory in Santiago, Chile. Capuchins are indigenous to South America.

While their early work was almost exclusively with monkeys and the great apes (particularly chimpanzees), gibbons became important recipients of MWARC rescue efforts in 2000. That year MWARC took in eight gibbons seized from illegal pet smugglers in Taiwan by the local authorities.

In 2001, working with agencies such as the Pingtung Rescue Centre for Endangered Wild Animals in Taiwan and the Cuc Phuong Endangered Primate Rescue Centre in Vietnam (established in 1993), the people from MWARC went to Vietnam to investigate the unlawful sale of gibbons in marketplaces. Owning and trading in endangered species such as gibbons is illegal in Vietnam, but it still happens. After a little searching, they found a baby female gibbon tied to a chicken cage. It was offered to them for U.S. $250, with the offer of a mate a week later. Elsewhere, they were told that a particular seller could get them three baby gibbons kept at his house for $250 each if they came the next day. When they returned, they were told by the seller that they could not film or take pictures of the young apes (as that might lead to the illegal owners being arrested). Several people were on the lookout for police as the deal went down and the MWARC staff members and their Vietnamese associates were presented with three baby gibbons all confined in one cage.

This type of situation presents a dilemma. Do you pay the asking price to obtain the gibbons, and guarantee that they will be saved? If you do that, you are supporting the black market in gibbons by adding to its illegal profits. Or, do you alert the police and hope for a successful raid and rescue sometime later? The problem with that option is that something could go horribly wrong, and the little animals would die as damning evidence of criminal activity.

In July 2001, three confiscated gibbons—Puma, an adult female black-handed gibbon, Kitty, a young female white-handed gibbon, and Pung-Yo (which in Mandarin means "friend"), a young male golden-cheeked gibbon—were destined for the centre. There they would be paired up with gibbons of their own species. But first they had to get there. They were sedated and put in boxes for transportation. Then the furry trio were first flown to Taipei, the capital city of Taiwan. After that, they had to endure a 14-hour flight to London. Fortunately, the flight was in a split passenger/cargo plane. The MWARC staff could regularly visit, calm, feed and water the young gibbon adventurers during the course of the flight. All the small apes arrived safe and well, if suffering a bit from jet lag.

PEANUT AND PUNG-YO OF THE MONKEY WORLD APE RESCUE CENTRE: ANOTHER HAPPY ENDING

Peanut, a female golden-cheeked gibbon, was born in or around 1998. She was smuggled from Vietnam to Thailand as an infant. She was then sold to a British bird and mammal smuggler who brought her illegally into England from Thailand. Fortunately, the smuggler was caught. Peanut was confiscated and brought to MWARC, where she arrived in the summer of 2000, still a very young gibbon child. Slightly less than a year later, she met Pung-Yo, whom as you have seen had his own sad early history. He is perhaps a year younger than Peanut. He was smuggled into Taiwan from his Vietnam birthplace, as another poor soul who would experience little gibbon parenting in his young life.

The plan was for them to breed, as part of what is called the European Breeding Programme. The pairing worked. They got along well from the beginning. Almost five years to the day after Pung-Yo's arrival at the park, on July 18, 2006, Peanut gave birth to Tien (which in Vietnamese means "angel, fairy, spirit or the first one"), a male. On February, 18, 2009, their second child, Tia Nang (which in Vietnamese means "ray of sunshine"), a daughter, was born. More recently, there has been the birth of their second son, Teo (a Vietnamese name said to mean "from tom,'" although that makes no sense to me) born on November 16, 2011.

What is particularly heartening about this story is the both Peanut and Pung-Yo, despite being stolen from their parents before they could be raised by them, have been able to become good parents themselves. Gibbons seem able to do that, as you have seen.

WILDLIFE FRIENDS FOUNDATION OF THAILAND

The Wildlife Friends Foundation of Thailand (WFFT) rescues individual gibbons in a number of circumstances. For instance, in Thailand, some people donate gibbons to Buddhist temples, as a way of being generous to the temples but also, possibly, to get rid of what may have been a pet whose sharp teeth and aggressiveness grew too much to handle. The monks dedicate many hours of each day to religion, and often don't have either the time or the ability to take good care of the gibbons in their charge. In 2012, the WFFT found and rescued a 12-year-old male pileated gibbon who had spent 10 years alone in a cage in a temple. More recently, they went to Patong Beach, the popular international tourist resort on the island of Phuket, having heard rumours that law enforcement officials were taking significant bribes to allow photographers with monkeys and gibbons props to go about their illegal business. The local government insisted this wasn't happening, but WFFT members took videos that proved the practice was still going strong. Two gibbons were rescued as a result.

BUILDING BRIDGES TO SAVE GIBBON LIVES

In the previous chapter, deforestation was noted as a major threat to gibbon survival. Too many trees were being cut down in the natural habitat of the small apes. The forest ranges of gibbons are being fragmented, forcing them to travel on the ground between feeding and sleeping locations. The question is: What can be done? The answer: Build bridges.

In an article entitled "Canopy Bridges: An Effective Conservation Tactic for Supporting Gibbon Populations in Forest Fragments," scientists J. Das, J. Biswas, P.C. Bhattacherjee and S. S. Rao tell the story of fragmented forests, drastically declining gibbon populations and a way to address the dilemma.

The area they were studying was Borajan Reserve, part of a wildlife sanctuary in the Assam region of northeastern India. Teacher's question: What kind of gibbons would be there? —Hoolocks, or course.

The Borajan Reserve is about five square kilometres in area. In 1995, about two-thirds of the forest in this reserve had what could be called a significant amount of canopy. Remember that canopy is very important to gibbons. It's where they sleep, often feed, and it is where they are safest from predators. Less canopy means more travelling, both in trees and on the ground. Travelling increases danger.

Four years later, only 30 percent—less than one-third—of the forest still had a significant amount of canopy. And the area where there was no forest at all had greatly increased. Forced to travel more often on the ground, gibbons found themselves in increased danger from predators. Infants and young gibbons relatively unskilled in climbing were more likely to fall and injure themselves just trying to reach the ground. All of this had a deadly effect. Between 1995 and 1999, 67% of the total gibbon population in the area was lost. The future did not look bright.

Then the bridge builders, who were sponsored by the Primate Research Centre in Assam, India came to the rescue. They constructed nine bridges made out of bamboo. All of these gibbon travel-aids were five metres off the ground. This was low enough so that the work could be done. Humans are a lot heavier than gibbons, so cannot safely work in the smaller branches higher up. Yet the bridges *were* high enough to be above the reach of most of the predators that gibbons had to worry about—for example, large cats, big snakes and domestic dogs.

The structures varied in length from seven to 21 metres, and were put in place on April 28, 2003. The first worry was whether or not the little apes would accept this man-made intrusion into their lives. That need not have been a concern. The gibbons started using the bridges in significant numbers on May 13, a little more than two weeks after they were installed. They liked them, and certainly preferred walking across them to moving on two feet on the ground. Gibbons—with the exception of Toga, whom we met in Chapter 5—don't fear heights; they fear lack of height, being on the ground.

What are advantages of these bridges? They save lives, particularly the lives of gibbon infants who could otherwise fall to their death, or be killed by ground-walking predators that are normally not a big threat to adult gibbons. The bridges are both cheap and easy to make. They can also be used as gibbon feeding stations, fast food for the commuting gibbons. Figs grow on lianas (woody vines), which can be attached to the bamboo poles used in the construction of the bridges. The bridges can also pay for themselves by encouraging increased ecotourism. Imagine what it would be like to watch gibbons travelling across a bamboo bridge, not hidden away in the canopy, but close enough that you could see them, and take pictures and videos of them. This is a good way to make gibbons visible.

Summing Up

As you've seen in this chapter, people are doing something to save the gibbons, all 17 species of them. (I suspect you have memorized that number by now.) These people include both those who live in gibbon countries in Asia, and those who make their homes far from where the small apes dwell in the wild. Some of them are people probably a lot like you.

There are a number of different ways in which someone can help the gibbons. *You* can help them in many different ways. Now that you've read this book, gibbons are no longer invisible to you. Make them visible to others. If you do, they will stay visible for a long time.

Books to Read about Gibbons

Do you want to read more about gibbons? Here are six very readable books about gibbons, the first and the last that are listed based on scientific fieldwork. All of them are both interesting and informative.

Thad Q. Bartlett, *The Gibbons of Khao Yai: Seasonal Variation in Behavior and Ecology*. Upper Saddle River, NJ: Pearson, 2009. While a scientific work and presenting some challenges to the non-scientific reader, this important work contains a good review of the history of gibbon study, and lets you know what it is like to study gibbons (in this case white-handed gibbons) in the wild.

Dilip Chetry, Rekha Chetry and P. C. Bhattacharjee, *Hoolock: The Ape of India*. Assam, India: Gibbon Conservation Centre, 2007. This isn't an easy book to get, but it presents a good introduction to hoolocks by three of the leading experts in gibbon study.

Mennakshi Negi Dufault, *Are You Ready for Love, Tomako?: The Story of a Cambodian Gibbon*. Frog Books, 2008. This book is very hard to find, but tells the story of one gibbon from the perspective of a gibbon; a good choice for younger readers.

Alice Schick, *The Siamang Gibbons: An Ape Family*. Milwaukee: Westwind Press, 1976. This is an easy-to-follow personal account of the lives of the siamangs Unk and Suzy, who are featured in our book.

Jeanne Ann Vanderhoef, *Gibbons in the Family Tree*. Lawrenceville, VA: Brunswick Press, 1996. This is a very readable, personal account of life with gibbons.

Tony Whitten, *The Gibbons of Siberut*. Toronto: J.M. Dent and Sons, 1982. Although written by a scientist, this is highly readable and charming. On the front cover the publishers rightly state that "This is the first full-length popular account of gibbon life."

Acknowledgements

Never has a book of mine owed so much to so many. First there is Angelika, my wife, who supported and worked on this project from the first day, when I said, "I am going to write a book about gibbons." Next, is David Stover, who was the first publisher with the insight to understand and believe in the vision that guided this book.

Then there are the gibbons themselves, the ones I got to know through observation, and in a few precious circumstances, through direct contact. Penelope, resident at the Bowmanville Zoo, is especially acknowledged, as she accepted me and gave me my first gibbon hug. I have to thank Stefanie McEwan for allowing me access to this wonderful little creature. All of the staff I encountered at the Bowmanville Zoo were very accommodating. This includes Sandra Brownelle, Andrew Cordier and Jacquie Rombough, and others whose names slipped out of my head. Then there is Bev Carter of the Toronto Zoo, Lana Borg of Safari Niagara and Cleo Kelly of the Elmvale Zoo. The staff from zoos in Canada, the United States, Britain and Australia were also very generous in the material that they shared with me.

Finally, there are the animals in my home life, who all keep me in touch with alternative ways of being: our parrots (the subject of my next book), our dogs, Wiikwaas and Trudy, and our cat, Brenda.

References

References are keyed by page number, with full details for each citation provided in the Bibliography.

CHAPTER ONE

Page 3: *Even Charles Darwin*: Darwin 2009: 556.

Page 4: *The Mogo Zoo in Australia*: www.mogozoo.com.au; as viewed on September 21, 2014.

Page 5: *As gibbon guru Thomas Geissmann*: Geissmann 2008.

Page 5: *They do not write books*: But see Lappan and Whittaker 2009 for a collection of state-of-the-science research papers.

Page 7: *It will be told in a more Western style*: For a more traditional type of telling, visit http://folklore-lover.blogspot.ca/2002/07/singing-ape-of-thailand.html or Chadchaidee 1994: 49–55.

Page 8: *Within this urn*: (http//.story-lovers.com/liststhailandstories. html.

CHAPTER TWO

Page 14: *To keep this in context*: www.thehumangenome.co.uk/THE_ HUMAN_GENOME/Primer.html.

Page 17: *In the gorges*: as quoted in Van Gulik 1967: 46.

Page 18: *The crane's call*: Van Gulik 1967: 54.

Page 21: *I may tell you moreover*: as quoted in Knox 1888: 434–35.

Page 22: *The Gibbon keeps himself*: Buffon 1785: 113.

Page 23: *In Thad Bartlett's thorough accounting*: Bartlett 2009: 69.

Page 23: Food chart: Clements 2002: 39.

Page 23: *Where there is a collection*: Carpenter 1964: 196.

Page 24: *On May 18, 1937*: Carpenter 1964: 188.

Pages 26–27: The story of the Vanderhoef gibbons and the zoo reunion is told in Vanderhoef 1996: 171–182.

Page 31: *By noting which hand*: Whitten 1982: 133.

CHAPTER THREE

Page 34: *We had been walking*: Bartlett 2009: xvii.

Page 41: *Schultz also remarked*: Schultz as quoted in Carpenter 1964: 148.

Page 41: *It seemed obvious to me*: Carpenter 1964: 200.

Page 43: *He does, however, groom more*: Bartlett 2009: 48.

Page 43: *. . . group movement appears*: Bartlett 2009: 101–02.

Page 44: *They are endowed*: Jardine 1866: 152.

Page 48: *Long, long ago*: Whitten 1982: 1.

Page 48: *It started with*: Whitten 1982: 35.

Page 49: *Then Bess*: Whitten 1982: 78.

Page 50: *Two whoops*: Kakati 1999.

Page 53: *I think of all*: Sterndale 1884.

Page 53: *The black gibbon*: Kipling 1904 [orig. 1891]: 58.

Page 54: *I first developed*: Bartlett 2009: 1.

Page 54: *Besides the specimens*: Raffles 1821: 242.

Page 56: *After several minutes*: Chivers 1974: 23.

Page 59: *Sometimes the silence*: Vassal 1910: 209.

Page 61: *Members of this "new" species*: Thinh et al. 2010.

CHAPTER FOUR

Page 66: *They walk erect*: Jardine 1866: 140–41.

Page 66: *. . . when they do occasionally*: Ingersoll 1907: 21.

Page 70: *I had total mama jitters* and subsequent two quotes: Ryan 2009: 251, 254, 256.

Page 73: *The two approaching animals*: Carpenter 1964: 245.

Page 79: *After detecting the presence*: Bartlett 2009: 104–05.

Page 79: *Among the antagonistic gestures*: Carpenter 1964: 246.

CHAPTER FIVE

Page 94: *I have a six-year-old female* and *I have little hope*: Schick and Schick 1976: 43.

Page 94: *The editorial comments*: Goodall 1990: 15.

Page 95: *The minute he saw her*: Gorski, April 1, 1960.

Page 95: *This seemed to work*: Mitchell 1962.

Page 96: *The zoo won an award*: Armstrong 1972.

Page 96: *During the fall*: Schick and Schick 1976: 73.

Page 98: *The young mother*: *Alive*, Fall 1991.

Page 98: *Having lost*: Herzog 1993.

Page 100: *Mary ran straight*: Clements 2002.

Page 101: *As I took a closer look*: Clements 2002: 39–40.

Page 101: *She had been imported*: January 1982.

Page 106: *I was amazed*: www.cbc.ca/canada/manitoba/story/2007/12/07/zoo-gibbon.html.

Page 106: *A recent study*: Suddendorf and Collier-Baker 2009.

Page 111: *Sure enough*: Whitten 1982: 121–22.

Page 112: *As I approached*: Whitten 1982: 136–37.

Page 112: *. . . she buried her face*: Whitten 1982: 142.

Page 113: *Box upon box*: Dufault 2008: 50.

Page 114: *Finally to Tomoko*: Dufault 2008: 153.

CHAPTER SIX

Page 119: *Gibbons' primary defense*: Clarke, Reichard and Zuberbühler 2012.

Page 123: *Catch, injure, care for*: Republic of Indonesia No. 5, 1990, p12.

Page 125: *The traveler in the Far East*: Carpenter 1964: 176.

Page 126: *The fate of these*: Carpenter 1964: 177.

CHAPTER SEVEN

Page 135: *When I closed my eyes*: Kazan 2012.

Bibliography

Armstrong, A. (1972, July 27). She set her mark on the zoo world. *Milwaukee Journal*.

Armstrong, A. (1985, February 11). Diabetes threatens apes' happiness. *Milwaukee Journal*.

Audebert, J.-B. (1798). *Histoire naturelle des Singes et des Makis*. Paris: Desray.

Aurélien Brulé. (n.d.). In *Discovery Nature Encyclopedia*. Retrieved from http://www.humanima.com/decouverte/en/article/aurelien-brule.

Bartlett, T. (2009). *The gibbons of Khao Yai: Seasonal variation in behavior and ecology*. Upper Saddle River, NJ: Pearson.

Beck, B. (1967). A study of problem solving by gibbons. *Behaviour, 28*(1–2), 95–109.

Brockelmann, W. (2009). Ecology and the social system of gibbons. In Lappan and Whittaker (Eds.), *The gibbons* (pp. 211–239). New York: Springer.

Brockelmann, W., et al. (2009). Census of eastern hoolock gibbons (*Hoolock leuconedys*) in Mahamyaing Wildlife Sanctuary, Sagaing Division, Myanmar. In Lappan and Whittaker (Eds.), *The gibbons* (pp. 435–451). New York: Springer.

[Buffon] Leclerc, G.-L., Comte de Buffon. (1766). Nomenclature of the apes. *Histoire Naturelle, 14*.

[Buffon] Leclerc, G.-L., Comte de Buffon. (1785). *Natural history, general and particular*. (Vol. 8). (W. Smellie, trans. and ed.) London: W. Strahan and T. Cadell.

Carpenter, C. (1940). A field study in Siam of the behavior and social relations of the gibbon (*Hylobates lar*). *Comparative Psychology Monographs, 16*, 1–201.

Carpenter, C. (1964). *Naturalistic behavior of nonhuman primates*. University Park, PA: The Pennsylvania State University Press.

CBC News (2007, December 7). *World's oldest grey gibbon dies in Winnipeg zoo*. Retrieved from http://www.cbc.ca/news/canada/manitoba/world-s-oldest-grey-gibbon-dies-at-winnipeg-zoo-1.667219

Chadchaidee, T. (1994). *Fascinating folktales of Thailand*. Google e-Books.

Chatterjee, H.J. (2009). Evolutionary relationships among the gibbons: A biogeographic perspective. In Lappan and Whittaker (Eds.), *The gibbons* (pp. 13–36). New York: Springer.

Cheney, D.L. and Seyfarth, R.M. (2007). *Baboon metaphysics: The evolution of a social mind*. Chicago: The University of Chicago Press.

Chetry, D., Chetry, R., Bhattacharjee, P.C. (2007). *Hoolock: The ape of India*. Assam, India: Gibbon Conservation Centre.

Cheyne, S.M. (2009). The role of reintroduction in gibbon conservation: Opportunities and challenges. In Lappan and Whittaker, *The gibbons* (pp. 477–496). New York: Springer.

Chivers, D. (1974). *The siamang in Malaya: A field study of a primate in tropical rain forest*. Berlin: S. Karger AG.

Clarke, E., Reichard, U., & Zuberbühler, K. (2012). The anti-predator behaviour of wild white-handed gibbons (*Hylobates lar*). *Behavior Ecology Sociobiology, 66,* 85–96.

Clements, D. (2003). *Postcards from the zoo: Animal tales from a 25-year zoo safari*. New York: HarperCollins.

Cunningham, C., Anderson, J.R., & Mootnick, A. (2006). Object manipulation to obtain a food reward in hoolock gibbons (*Bunopithecus hoolock*). *Animal Behaviour, 71,* 621–629.

Cutting, S.C. (2009). Gabriella's gibbon. *Gibbon Journal*.

Dallmann, R., & Geissmann, T. (2009). Individual and geographical variability in the songs of wild silvery gibbons (*Hylobates moloch*) on Java, Indonesia. In Lappan and Whittaker (Eds.), *The gibbons* (pp. 91–110). New York: Springer.

Darwin, C. (2009: orig. 1874). *The descent of man and selection in relation to sex*. Cambridge: Cambridge University Press.

Das, J., Biswas, J., Bhattacherjee, P., & Mohnot, S.M. (2009). The distribution and abundance of hoolock gibbons in India. In Lappan and Whittaker (Eds.), *The gibbons* (pp. 409–433). New York: Springer.

Das, J., Biswas, J., Bhattacherjee, P.C., & Rao, S.S. (2009). Canopy bridges: An effective conservation tactic for supporting gibbon populations in forest fragments. In Lappan and Whittaker, (Eds.), *The gibbons* (pp. 467-475). New York: Springer.

D'Ath, J. (2013). The singing ape. *The Lost World Circus*, no. 2.

Davis, W. (2007). *Light at the edge of the world*. Vancouver: Douglas and McIntyre.

Dufault, M.N. (2008). *Are you ready for love, Tomako?: The story of a Cambodian gibbon*. Frog Books.

Elder, A. (2009). Hylobatid diets revisited: The importance of body mass, fruit availability, and interspecific competition. In Lappan and Whittaker (Eds.), *The gibbons* (pp. 133–159). New York: Springer.

Ferguson, G. (n.d.). *The human gene: Poems on the book of life*. Retrieved from www.the humangenome.co.uk/THE_HUMAN_GENOME/Primer.html.

Feeroz, M.M., & Islam, M.A. (1992). Ecology and behaviour of hoolock gibbons of Bangladesh. *Primates, 33*(4), 451–464.

Fight for life: 6 ounce ape born prematurely at zoo. (1967, May 31). *Milwaukee Journal.*

Fischer, W. (1966). *Das Jahr mit den Gibbons.* Wittenberg: A. Zimsen Verlag.

Geissmann, T. (1989). A female black gibbon, *Hylobates concolor* subspecies, from northeastern Vietnam. *International Journal of Primatology, 10*(5), 455–476.

Geissmann, T. (2009). Door slamming: Tool-use by a captive white-handed gibbon (*Hylobates lar*). *Gibbon Journal 5*, 53–59.

Goodall, J. (1990). *Through a window: 30 years observing the Gombe chimpanzees.* Boston: Houghton Mifflin.

Gorski, H.V. (1960, 1 April). Bride from Sumatra is something of an ape. *Milwaukee Journal.*

Gould, S.J. (1996: orig. 1981). *The mismeasure of man.* New York: W. W. Norton.

Gray, S. (n.d.) Conservation difficulties for *Hylobates lar*: White-handed gibbons and Thailand's illegal pet trade.

Herzog, K. (1993, 10 December). Zoo ape in full swing as foster mother: Siamang, baby getting along. *Milwaukee Sentinel.*

Herzog, K. (1994, April 27). Suzy may wind up in museum. *Milwaukee Sentinel.*

Hirai, H., Hanyano, A., Tanaka, H., Mootnick, A., Wijayanto, H., & Perwitasari-Farajallah, D. (2009). Genetic differentiation of agile gibbons between Sumatra and Kalimantan in Indonesia. In Lappan and Whittaker (Eds.) *The gibbons* (pp. 37–49). New York: Springer.

Holubitsky, J. (2008, January 10). Hand-raising baby gibbon a labour of love for zookeeper. *Edmonton Journal.* Retrieved from www.canada.com/story_print.html?id=ddc1ce79-cd9b-4ff6-b395-81 39882aa3e7&s.

http://folklore-lover.blogspot.ca/2002/07/singing-ape-of-thailand.html.

Ingersoll, E. (1907). *The life of animals: The mammals.* (2nd ed.) London: Macmillan.

International Primate Protection League. (1976, March). *Newsletter, 2*(3). Retrieved from www.ippl.org/newsletter/1970s/007_v2_n3_1975-02.pdf.

International Primate Protection League. (1975, October). *Newsletter, 3*(1). Retrieved from www.ippl.org/newsletter/1970s/008_v3_n1_1976-03.pdf.

International Primate Protection League. (1976, September). *Newsletter, 3*(2). Retrieved from www.ippl.org/newsletter/1970s/008_v3_n2_1976-03.pdf.

International Primate Protection League. (1982, January). *Newsletter, 9*(1). Retrieved from www.ippl.org/newsletter/1980s/027_v09_n1_1982-01.pdf.

International Primate Protection League. (1982, May). *Newsletter, 9*(2). Retrieved from www.ippl.org/newsletter/1980s/09_n2_1982-05.pdf.

International Primate Protection League. (1999, April). *Newsletter, 26*(1). Retrieved from www.ippl.org/newsletter/1990s/_v26_n1_1999-04.pdf.

International Primate Protection League. (2001, April). *Newsletter, 28*(1). Retrieved from www.ippl.org/newsletter/2000s/083_v28_n1_2001-04.pdf.

International Primate Protection League. (2006, December). *Newsletter, 33*(3). Retrieved from www.ippl.org/newsletter/2000s/100 v33_n3_2006-12.pdf.

International Primate Protection League. (2011, September) *Newsletter, 38*(2). Retrieved from www.ippl.org/newsletter/2010s/112_v39_n2_2011-09.pdf.

International Primate Protection League. (2012, June 26). Igor's 25th anniversary at IPPL. Retrieved from www.ippl.org/gibbon/igors-25th-anniversary-at-ippl/.

International Primate Protection League. (2014). History: Reasons to support IPPL. Retrieved from www.ippl.org/gibbon/about-us/history-reasons-to-support-ippl.

International Primate Protection League. (2014). IPPL's gibbon sanctuary. Retrieved from www.ippl.org/gibbon/ippls-gibbon-sanctuary/arun-rangsi.

Jablonski, N., & Chaplin, G. (2009). The fossil record of gibbons. In Lappan and Whittaker (Eds.), *The gibbons,* (pp. 111–130). New York: Springer.

Jardine, W. (1866). *The naturalist's library: Mammalia, the natural history of monkeys.* (Vol. 27.) London: Henry G. Bohn.

Johnson, A., Singh, S., Duandala, M., & Hedemark, M. (2005). The western black crested gibbon *Nomascus concolor* in Laos: New records and conservation status. *Oryx, 39*(3), 311–317.

Kakati, K. (1999). The singing apes: Kashmira Kakati studies the world of the hoolock gibbons in the Borajam reserve in Assam. *Frontline, 16*(3).

Kazan, D. (2012). Kazan today: A recipe for success. Retrieved from www.kazantoday.com/WeeklyArticles/alanmootnick.html.

Keith, S.A., Walker, M.S., & Geissmann, T. (2009). Vocal diversity of Kloss's gibbons (*Hylobates klossii*) in the Mentawai Islands, Indonesia. In Lappan and Whittaker (Eds.), *The gibbons,* (pp. 51–71). New York: Springer.

Kipling, J.L. (1904: orig. 1891). *Beast and man in India: A popular sketch of Indian animals in their relation to the people.* Retrieved from www.gutenberg.org/ebook.

Knox, T.W. (1888). *The travels of Marco Polo for boys and girls.* New York: Putnam's Sons.

Lappan, S. (2009). Patterns of infant care in wild siamangs (*Symphalangus syndactylus*) in Southern Sumatra. In Lappan and Whittaker (Eds.), *The gibbons,* (pp. 327–345). New York: Springer.

Lappan, S., & Whittaker, D.J. (Eds.). (2009). *The gibbons: New perspectives on small ape socioecology and population biology.* New York: Springer.

Mitchell, D. (1962, July 11). Birth of a siamang here called first in captivity. *Milwaukee Journal.*

Mogo Zoo. (n.d.). Retrieved from www.mogozoo.com.au.

Monda, K., Simmons, R.E., Kressirer, P., Su, B., & Woodruff, D. (2007). Mitochondrial DNA hypervariable region-1 sequence variation and phylogeny of the concolor gibbons, Nomascus. *American Journal of Primatology, 60,* 1285–1306.

Mootnick, A. (1984). Census of gibbons in North America. In Preuschoft, Chivers, Brockelmann & Creel (Eds.), *The lesser apes: Evolutionary and behavioural biology*, (pp. 61–73). Edinburgh: Edinburgh University Press.

Mootnick, A. (2006). Gibbon (Hylobatidae) species identification recommended for rescue or breeding centers. *Primate Conservation, 21*, 103–138.

Mootnick, A., & Groves, C.P. (2005). A new generic name for the Hoolock gibbon (Hylobatidae). *International Journal of Primatology, 26*, 971–976.

Nadler, T., Ngoc, V., Thanh, & Streicher, U. (2007). Conservation status of Vietnamese primates. *Vietnamese Journal of Primatology, 1*, 7–26.

Nijman, V., Martinez, Y., & Shepherd, C.R. (2009). Saved from trade: Donated and confiscated gibbons in zoos and rescue centres in Indonesia. *Endangered Species Research, 9*, 151–57.

O'Brian, P. (1972). *Post Captain*. London: Collins.

Poyas, A., & Bartlett, T. (2008). Infant development in a captive white-cheeked gibbon (*Nomascus leucogenys*). *American Journal of Primatology, 70 (supplement)*, 1098–1145.

Raffles, T.S. (1821). Descriptive catalogue of a zoological collection, made on account of the Honourable East India Company in the island of Sumatra and its vicinities, under the direction of Sir Thomas Stamford Raffles, Lieutenant Governor of Fort Marlborough with additional notices illustrative of the natural history of those countries. *Transactions of the Linnean Society, 13*, 239–274.

Rawson, B., Clements, T., & Hor, N.M. (2009). Status and conservation of yellow-cheeked crested gibbons (*Nomascus gabriellae*) in the Selma Biodiversity Conservation Area, Mondulkiri Province, Cambodia. In Lappan and Whittaker (Eds.), *The gibbons* (pp. 387–408). New York: Springer.

Reichard, U. (2009). The social organization and mating system of Khao Yai white-handed gibbons: 1992–2006. In Lappan and Whittaker (Eds.), *The gibbons* (pp. 347–384). New York: Springer.

Ryan, J. (2009). *Amazing animals: Inspiring stories about the bond between humans and animal*. Edmonton: Folklore Publishing.

Sapolsky, R. (2002). *A primate's memoir*. New York: Touchstone Books.

Schick, A. (1976). *The siamang gibbons: An ape family*. Milwaukee: Westwind Press.

Schultz, A. (1939). *Notes on disease and healed fractures of wild apes and their bearing on the antiquity of pathological conditions in man*. Baltimore: Johns Hopkins University Press.

Siamang fights for life at zoo. (1972, February 7). *Milwaukee Sentinel*.

Siminiski, J. (n.d.). Earthkeeper hero: Dr. Shirley McGreal. Retrieved from www.miheroes.org/print.asp?hero=s_mgreal.

Smitty the baby ape cuts apron strings. (1967, September 28). *Milwaukee Journal*.

Steckley, J.L. (2011). *Introduction to physical anthropology*. Toronto: Oxford University Press.

Sterndale, R.A. (1884). *Natural history of the mammalia of India and Ceylon.* Calcutta: Thacker Spink and Co.

Suddendorf, T., & Collier-Baker, E. (2009). The evolution of primate visual self-recognition: Evidence of absence in lesser apes. *Proceedings of the Royal Society: Biological Sciences, 276* (1662), 1671–1677.

Thinh, V. N., Mootnick, A.R., Thanh, V.N., Nadler, T., & Roos, C. (2010). A new species of crested gibbon, from the central Annamite mountain range. *Vietnamese Journal of Primatology, 1*(4), 1–12.

Vanderhoef, J.A. (1996). *Gibbons in the family tree.* Lawrenceville, VA: Brunswick Press.

Van Gulik, R.H. (1967). *The gibbon in China: An essay in Chinese animal lore.* New York: E. J. Brill Archive.

Vassal, G. (1910). *On and off duty in Annam.* London: William Heinemann.

Wee Natale, Yule baby, dies at zoo. (1964, December 30). *Milwaukee Sentinel.*

Whittaker, D.J. (2009). Saving the small apes: Conservation assessment of gibbon species at the 2006 Asian Primate Red List Workshop. In Lappan and Whittaker (Eds.), *The gibbons* (pp. 497–499). New York: Springer.

Whittaker, D.J., & Lappan, S. (2009). The diversity of small apes and the importance of population-level studies. In Lappan and Whittaker (Eds.), *The gibbons* (pp. 3–10). New York: Springer.

Whitten, T. (1982). *The gibbons of Siberut.* Toronto: J.M. Dent and Sons.

Wildlife Friends Foundation Thailand. (2013, February 22). Phuket still hell for "protected" wildlife. Retrieved from http://www.wfft.org/primates/phuket-still-hell-for-protected-wildlife/.

Zoological society of Milwaukee County. Surrogate siamang. (1991, Fall). *Alive,* 12–14.

Index